CAPSTONE
A Wiley Brand

Dream It, Do It, Live It

9 Easy Steps to Making Things Happen for You

Richard Newton and Ciprian Adrian Rusen

Illustrations by Laura Dumitru

WILEY

© 2013 Richard Newton and Ciprian Adrian Rusen

Registered office

Capstone Publishing Ltd. (A Wiley Company), John Wiley and Sons Ltd, The Atrium, Southern Gate, Chichester, West Sussex, PO19 8SQ, United Kingdom

For details of our global editorial offices, for customer services and for information about how to apply for permission to reuse the copyright material in this book please see our website at www.wiley.com.

Library of Congress Cataloging-in-Publication Data to follow

A catalogue record for this book is available from the British Library.

ISBN 978-0-857-08456-9 (paperback) ISBN 978-0-857-08455-2 (ebk)

ISBN 978-0-857-08454-5 (ebk) ISBN 978-0-857-08453-8 (ebk)

Illustrations by Laura Dumitru

Set in 9/13.5 pt Helvetica Neue LT Std by Toppan Best-set Premedia Limited

Printed in Great Britain by TJ International Ltd, Padstow, Cornwall, UK

To those who dare to follow their dreams, no matter how hard they are.

CONTENTS

Why Read this Book: What's It about and How will It Help You?

Here is a simple model for achieving dreams. Maybe you have a dream, but do not know how to achieve it, or maybe you want help or just a bit of structure to start living your dream. Either way, this book is for you.

The approach in this book works. It is based on well tested principles and approaches used all over the world by project managers and other professionals whose job it is to make things happen. We have taken the most useful tools, advice and experiences and distilled them into a concise, practical guide for everyone. There is some explicit theory in this book, but much more is hidden below the surface.

The book is a tool. It can be referred to repeatedly as you make your way towards your dreams. We like the fact you dream, but we want to take you further – from dreaming it, through doing it, to living it.

The approach in this book has been used in real life. The book includes real-life examples and dreams of people who have applied the steps as they are described. Four normal people had the courage to share their dreams with us, apply our recommendations and share their learning and experience. Their personal adventures are one of the most useful parts of the book.

The advice is easy to understand and apply. This is not a long book, but it includes the most important principles you need, the most important questions to ask yourself, and the most important steps to follow in an easy to use format.

Reading this Book

This book is written as a guide for anyone who dreams and really wants their dreams to become reality. It is a workbook that will act as your mentor as you go through the process of achieving your dream. The guidance is based on the 9 step approach we have designed based on our experiences, to help everyone achieve their dreams.

Each of the 9 steps has a chapter which we suggest you read through and then work on your dream. There is an important word in the last sentence – *work*. Because this book does not pretend there is some magic that can make you achieve your dreams by belief alone. Achieving your dream takes effort, but it is the sort of effort that everyone can do if they go about it in the right way. This book shows you the right way. It is realistic, achievable and friendly.

Of course, you can read the book end-to-end in one sitting. It's not an overly long book. However, we suggest you don't think of it like a novel to be experienced, but treat it as a tool. And like a tool, you should read it as you progress and when you need to use it. If you are the sort of person who likes to be really thorough, and wants to get the most from this book, we suggest you do the following:

1. Go through the book quickly once – scanning all the chapters so you understand the sequence of events we are going to take you through.
2. Work with the book on your dream. Take each chapter, one at a time, and only move onto the next chapter when you know you have completed the work required. There is a section in each chapter called "How will I know I've done well", which is there to help you understand when it is time to move onto the next chapter.
3. Use the book again and again as a reference source when you work on other dreams in future. At the end of each chapter is a very short section titled "Questions to ask yourself". These questions provide a way of checking you understand the advice in the chapter. They are also a quick reference to use once you are

familiar with the book, that you can come back to again and again.

The chapters are in a deliberate order starting with working out what your dream really is, all the way through to what to do once you have achieved it.

The chapters have two main parts. The first part is our advice: what we suggest you do at each stage of your dream. After this are the case studies. These are the stories of four real people, following their actual dreams, using the approach that we describe in this book. We worked with them whilst we wrote the book. We think of these people as our heroes. We introduce our heroes in the next section of this book. To give you a flavour of the dreams:

- One concerns getting a doctoral degree which involves a research project, getting people involved, finding funding and many other challenges.
- The next concerns someone who wants to become a singer, for the best of all reasons: she loves singing!
- The final dream brings two people together who want to start their own business.

These are the real dreams of real people. People like us, people like you, people who had a dream, and who have achieved it.

Each of these case studies is based on at least one interview we held with each of our heroes, for each stage of our approach. These are really worth reading. They not only bring the approach to life, but each of our heroes has built on and extended our approach and provide their own ideas and advice for achieving dreams.

Your very first step is to get familiar with our heroes, and then read the first chapter – Dream. At this stage you need nothing else other than a willingness to read those few pages. When you have done that, you will have already started on the journey to achieving your dream.

A Little Bit About Us

We both are successful people who have achieved dreams. We've made lots of mistakes and we've learnt from them. We've achieved things we are proud of and we've raised the bar for ourselves. And we know lots of other successful people who have inspired and influenced us in writing this book. We don't claim to be gurus or visionaries, but we do claim that we know how to get things done. It's not magic, it's not rocket science, but it is powerful. We share it with you in this book.

The book is based on our own experiences, achieving our personal dreams as well as managing challenging projects for multinational companies. We both dreamt of becoming published authors – and we both are. We have climbed steep mountains, travelled to exotic places, started a successful consultancy company, broken a world record and much, much more. Our successful business projects were worth millions of dollars. Some had high probabilities of failure and impacted the lives of many people. We were lucky enough to do well as project managers and deliver the results expected of us. But this is not only about the big stuff. We've also achieved little dreams that matter to no-one else other than to ourselves. They are just as important.

We have each, independently, written and published books before, but it's the first time we have written a book quite like this. We've done our best to make it as useful and fun to read as possible. We were lucky to meet some great people along the way, some of whom agreed to be guests in our book and share their dreams with us and with you. Others made awesome illustrations which make the book look and feel warm and friendly. We're happy with the end result. We hope it helps you. Enjoy!

Your friendly guides to achieving your dreams,

Richard Newton   **Ciprian Adrian Rusen**

MEET OUR HEROES

Alex is a very ambitious undergraduate student, in his final year of medicinal studies. He loves to dream big and the dream he chose to share with us is very ambitious: he wants to get a doctoral degree which involves coordinating a complex research project, getting lots of people involved, receiving private or public funding and many other challenges worthy of an experienced project manager. The only downside is that that he is not a project manager and he doesn't have any project management studies. He is only a medical student. Will he be able to pull it off? To find out, read his story, chapter by chapter. His adventure is full of surprises, ups and downs and lessons that are useful to everyone with an ambitious dream to make real.

Olive has spent most of her career working in the world of newspapers and online magazines. She loved the thrill of being among the first to cover the latest breaking news and the variety of each day spent in the office. And yet, there's one thing that bothers her: apart from taking care of her career, she did not spend any valuable time working on the more personal dreams of hers. Those things that won't bring her a great deal of financial gain or any special social status, but would make her feel happier and more whole as a human being. She decided to do something about it and shares her first adventure with us in making an old and personal dream come true: that of becoming a bar singer.

Anna has had several successful careers. She originally studied languages, and then trained as an animator. She worked on animations for several years, on the production of a range of TV series and advertisements, with a specialization in natural history animation. Then she retrained to follow one of the passions in her life – herbal medicine. After qualifying as a medical herbalist Anna set up a practice in the UK, which she still runs successfully treating patients with a range of conditions. Outside of work, Anna has a wide variety of pastimes including travel, mountaineering, wood and stone carving, as well as many design interests. She is a published author and a mother. She started her design business with Amelia about a year ago, and it is the story of this nascent business she shared with us.

Amelia is an artist and art teacher. She originally trained as a textile designer. Amelia designs, creates and works on her art in multiple forms and media, taking inspiration from a wide variety of sources. She has travelled widely, observing and exploring different artistic heritages. She is an inspirational art teacher who has started many of her students on successful artistic careers. Her works have been enjoyed for a long time by family and friends, and were the original trigger for the design business which she set up with Anna about a year ago, having dreamt of making wider use of her creative skills. Outside of work, Amelia loves skiing and running. She is also known to her family and friends as a great cook. Anna and Amelia are sisters-in-law.

1   DREAM

All our dreams can come true – if we have the courage to pursue them.

Walt Disney

The Goal

What do people like Steve Jobs, Mahatma Gandhi and Walt Disney have in common? As well as being icons of their generations, they were passionate, relentless dreamers. And they had a habit of turning dreams into reality. Even when a dream became reality, they did not stop there. They constantly refined dreams to make them better and closer to what they really wanted, and they kept dreaming new dreams to pursue and achieve.

The key element that gave them a shot at being successful was their dreams. In this chapter we will encourage you to dream more and help you become a focused dreamer. You too can turn your most important dreams into reality, just like Steve Jobs, Mahatma Gandhi and Walt Disney. Feeling excited?

Dreams Are Diverse

Depending on who you ask about dreams, from psychology professors to fortune tellers to the people you know, you will end up with different answers. What everyone will agree, is that dreams are diverse and can be split into many categories, based on multiple criteria. Here are some of the most common types of dreams:

- After a demanding day, we dream about what we've done, rehashing the events of the day and tying up loose ends.
- Dreams can be recurring, telling the same story over and over again. Or they may simply continue the same story they started a while ago, as if we have a story teller in our head, trying to tell us something important.

- Sometimes we dream about our past and what we could have done differently.
- We dream about things we would like to have.
- Some of us dream about colours, fantasy worlds and characters we have never met in our lives.
- Sometimes we dream about breakthrough changes that would make for an amazing life or about disasters that would turn our life into a living hell.

Looking at all these types of dreams, one can't help wonder: what do you do with them? Dreams are like a library of apparently crazy ideas of what you can do with your life. Dreaming is great and can fuel your life with inspiration on what to do next. But which dreams really matter? Which dreams are worth focusing on?

The Dreams that Matter

First of all, the dreams that will change your life for the better are always looking forward, to what can be, not what was. If some of your dreams are about changing the past, then simply don't dwell on them. They are not dreams that will help you change and become a successful person. Your future is what matters, not your past. The future is what energizes people, not the past. Thomas Jefferson once smartly said: *"I like dreams of the future better than the history of the past."*

Only a few dreams are really important. And, if you can't point them out with ease, then take some time to think and ask yourself:

- Which dreams are about things I would like to do?
- Which dreams are about what I would like to be as a professional?

- Which dreams are about who I would like to become as a person?
- Which dreams are about bringing change to the world around me?
- Which of them are the most reoccurring – older ideas and stories that have nagged me for some time?
- Which dreams, if achieved, would make me happiest?

Briefly write down the list of your dreams. While doing this, you will notice that:

- You dream a lot more than you think and that's great. Don't stop dreaming!
- Some dreams have a common theme. For example, a dream about becoming a different person may mean that you must choose a different profession and also do certain things that will help along the road – all of which you might have dreamed already.
- Some dreams are very big in the sense that they are about huge changes that seem almost impossible to turn into reality.
- Some dreams are hard to define in detail. They are strong, always sitting in the back of your head, but feel generic and hard to pin down to specifics.

While reading the list, your gut will start to tell you which dreams are important and which are not. If any of the dreams on the list don't stir up any emotions and leave you pretty much indifferent, then you just gave yourself the OK to remove them from the list. If some dreams feel scary, too big to be true and yet really exciting, that's great. Keep them on your list!

There will be dreams which fire your imagination and make it go places, adding more details to the dream, making it bigger or better. Make sure you keep these dreams, no matter how big or how small they are.

Now that you have your list of dreams and ideas worth pursuing, you need to pick one and stick with it for a while. This book will help you achieve challenging dreams, bigger than the ones you've accomplished so far. However, if you don't feel like starting big, that's OK. It is important that you start somewhere. If you are feeling scared of starting to work on your big dreams, simply choose one which feels doable, less complicated and daunting. Once you've gone through this book and made that dream a reality, your courage will grow and you will feel like taking on bigger challenges and turning them into reality.

Stick to One Dream

People are unique beings. Some people have the same dream over and over while others have too many and switch between them with incredible ease. Other people have a few constant dreams, which stay with them for a long time.

You might argue that some people work on more than one dream at a time and that's true. If you do the same, that's great and we encourage you to keep doing that. However, to make sure you understand the model presented in this book and you achieve more than in the past, we encourage you to pick one dream and use it to experiment and learn our model. Do not worry about applying the model we propose to all of today's important dreams. Once you get the first nailed down, you can experiment and apply the model to more than one dream, and work on several in parallel.

If you are the type of person who leaps easily from dream to dream and doesn't really stick to one, we gently suggest that you pick an important dream you've identified earlier and do your best to stick to it while going through this book. As you will learn later, it is OK to refine the details of a dream, add more detail to it and make it even better. It is not OK to switch to another dream midway, or to change the direction of a dream in a dramatic way, unless it is the result of what you have learnt or you need to adapt to a changing context.

Constantly switching between dreams will end up with you achieving nothing. Therefore, try to be as disciplined as you can and stick to one dream for the whole duration of the book. If you choose your dream carefully and apply the model we are sharing, you will be successful. You will get into the habit of choosing one dream at a time and sticking to it until it gets done.

People who are widely successful might not be disciplined in the way they act and make their dreams a reality, but they are stubborn when it comes to their dreams. They stick to them and don't stop until they become reality. Do your best and try to be as stubborn as they are.

Dream the Dream

Now you are really getting close to actually working on the dream you have chosen. Before you do that, you need to do a bit more dreaming. Take that dream and think about it as often as you can. Try to imagine, feel, taste and smell the outcome. Do it until you can really visualize the dream and its outcome. This is very helpful especially with big dreams, which are usually a bit generic and not well defined.

Moving away from a generic dream of "I want to be rich", to a well-defined dream of "I want to create my own company that makes 300,000 US dollars a year, by creating customized office furniture and equipment for companies with unusual work environments" makes a huge difference in having a shot at being successful. It is really important to know what your life will be like when you achieve this dream; understand what the outcome you desire is.

Tackling Big Dreams

Depending on your context and the type of person you are, you might choose a very big dream you want to accomplish. The kind of dream that would take years of work but, when done, would be the most amazing thing in your life. Some ambitious examples are: creating a company which earns its first million in three years, moving to a different continent and starting a completely new life, getting accepted on an MBA programme of a famous foreign university, becoming a famous scientist, movie actor or any kind of star, etc. It doesn't matter what dream it is, if it takes you more than a year to do it, then it is a big dream which you should handle differently than dreams which take a few months to accomplish.

When you focus on such a big dream, try to think about smaller elements which, when placed together, take you to where you want to be. Call them your "must do" mini-dreams, the dots that, when connected, will make your big dream come true. Let's take the example we mentioned earlier: "I want to create my own company that makes 300,000 US dollars a year, by creating customized office furniture and equipment for companies with unusual work environments". This is a very ambitious dream which (for most people) would take more than a year to complete. The dream is composed of at least three smaller dreams: the one of creating the company, the dream of starting the company in a successful way and the dream of getting to the yearly profit of 300,000 US dollars. Identifying these big elements that make the big dream is very important, as you need to choose the first element as being your first dream, work on getting it accomplished, then work on the second dream and finally, once the second is in place, on the third and ultimate dream.

Why do we recommend this approach for tackling big dreams? Because big dreams are scary, complex and hard to make a reality. Just thinking about them can make you paralyzed and unable to start. Identifying smaller dreams, that take you where you want to be, is a healthy exercise that:

- Will make you feel more confident. Splitting a big dream into smaller pieces, which are less complex to handle, will make you feel more relaxed about starting to work on them.
- Will increase your chances of success. Working on a smaller dream, means you will have an easier time making it come true. Also, what you learn from each small dream will come in handy when working on the ones that follow. With each small dream, you will get better at accomplishing the big one you had in the first place.
- Gives you something you can practically work on and achieve. A big dream is great, but even the biggest dreams are realized by small, tangible actions. If the dream is very big, it can be hard to break it down into actual steps you should follow. The answer is to do one bit at a time, whilst not forgetting that each smaller dream leads onto the next dream.

Have you chosen a big dream to follow? If you have, identify the smaller dreams which take you there and choose to focus on the first dream of all of them. Dream that smaller dream for a while, before you move to the next step.

How will I Know I've Done Well?

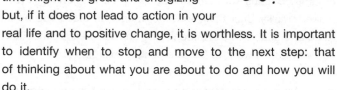

Being in a state of dreaming all the time might feel great and energizing but, if it does not lead to action in your real life and to positive change, it is worthless. It is important to identify when to stop and move to the next step: that of thinking about what you are about to do and how you will do it.

There are three important factors in identifying if dreaming is productive or not:

- **You can visualize the dream.** If you can really imagine the outcome of your dream and formulate to yourself what your life will look and feel like once you've achieved it, then you are almost done dreaming.
- **You are able to share the dream with others.** If you are able to visualize the dream, you should be able to share it with others. Talk briefly about the dream with some of the people you trust and see if they can understand it and visualize it based on what you share with them. They don't have to agree with it, just understand it. If they can, that's great. You should move immediately to the next stage. If they cannot understand it and visualize it, you should either spend more time crystallizing the dream, clarifying the bits about the outcome that are

hard to understand or, move to the next step but keep in mind that you might have a hard time getting people to follow and help out. You may need to spend more time in the next stage ironing out more details.

- **You are not spending too much time on dreaming.** If you are spending too many days dreaming, then you are in trouble. You will not get anything done and you are simply wasting your time. That can be due to choosing completely the wrong dream, one that doesn't really inspire you, lacking importance for your success and well-being. Or, it can simply be because it is too ambitious and you are not yet ready to tackle it. In both cases you should change the dream and go over again through the exercise presented in this chapter. In case you chose to focus on a very big dream that needs a lot of time to clarify, choose a smaller one to focus on for now and leave the big dream in the back of your head. As you get things done, other dreams will become clearer.

Now that you have a great dream to follow, it is time to think about what you are about to do and how. Doesn't it feel exciting? You are on your way to achieving a dream. But first, let's see how dreaming works for others. We have a few interesting people you need to meet.

What Our Heroes Say

Alex

We met with Alex in a small restaurant, close to the places where he spends most of his time: the study quarters of his university and the med-lab where he does most of his research and experimentation. Our aim was to get to know more about the way he dreams and how he chooses the dreams that matter most to him.

1. What kind of a dreamer are you?

For starters, I don't really have many dreams that stick with me for a long time. I just have a few big dreams I really want to achieve. They both evolved from a dream that started when I was in high school.

Back then, I was in a class which focused mostly on studying maths and programming. I really liked these fields of study and I was good at them. I thought at that point that it would be good for me to study IT at some big university. However, I did not have a clear dream or vision of what I really wanted to do with my life. I was simply assuming that would be a good next step for me, since everybody else thought the same.

I was lucky that I had a close relationship with a physics professor. He knew me quite well and we talked about lots of subjects, including what would be a good next step for me to go for in life. He shared with me his passion for medicine and what it means to be a doctor, both for the person who practises the profession and the patients who benefit from it. This really got me thinking about what I should do with my life.

As I learned more about medicine, both from our conversations and the things I read up on this field, I became more drawn to it. I also analyzed myself and realized how I always tend to be the one who listens to the worries of friends and family, who tries to calm down people when they are upset or who is simply there and listening when needed. I always liked the closeness and intimacy of such moments and I realized I would love to help people by being a doctor. The more I thought about it, the more I could imagine myself doing this, much more than being the "IT guy". So here I am today, in my final years of study, learning as much as I can about medicine.

2. But what about being good at maths and programming? Did you ditch the dream of being an IT guy?

Yes . . . but not completely. Another realization I had was that I can easily learn most things I need to know related to computers and technology. I don't have to go to university for that. Today I am one of those medicine students who really understand technology and can use computers, robots, scanners and other technical devices used in medical research and analysis with relative ease. Even though I chose not to follow a career in IT, I can still use my inclinations for this field and apply them in medicine.

3. True. Sounds like you've made a good choice. Let's get back to those few big dreams you mentioned. Can you share them with us?

Yes of course. There are two big dreams which take most of my time and energy:

The first, is becoming a Medical Educator, teaching what people working in this field would call evidence-based medicine. This is a doctor who learns both by practising medicine for the benefit of his patients and by trying to teach students based on his theoretical and practical knowledge. Each patient becomes a new opportunity for study, and as such you get to know the person and propose treatments proven to be effective for his/her specific needs. As the treatment progresses, you closely monitor the patient's evolution and adjust treatment on the basis of efficacy.

The second is becoming a Physician Scientist, practising what other doctors would call bench-to-bed medicine. It is like being both a doctor but also a scientist. This is a special type of medicine that tries to integrate the newest information available with standard medical care. You get to help people not just by applying standard medical knowledge.

4. They both sound exciting. If you were to choose one to stick with and work at making it happen, which would it be?

    That's my biggest problem. Why should I pick only one? No matter how much I think about it, I cannot choose one over the other and I would really love to make them both happen.

5. But would you really have the time and energy to work on them both, successfully? They are both very big, complex dreams and this doesn't sound realistic.

    True, working on both these dreams in parallel would be too much. However, I really don't want to give up on one over the other. I thought about this for some time and I think the best approach for me would be to first work on my second dream, that of becoming a Physician Scientist, and then on the first dream I shared.

Doing it in this order is best, as becoming a Physician Scientist will give me a wider range of knowledge and experiences than a standard medical career. Doing this for a few years would give me the edge required to become a very good Doctor and Medical Educator later on.

I do need to pick one first and it will be the dream of becoming a Physician Scientist. Let's see how this adventure goes.

6. Speaking of becoming a Physician Scientist – looking at where you are today, this is a big dream which will take you a few years to accomplish. Which are the most important elements (smaller dreams) that will take you there?

There are quite a few big elements I need to do first, before I can actually become a Physician Scientist. I've recently started to work on the first thing I need to get done, which is to choose a medical specialization and earn a doctoral degree in that specialization.

7. Is it OK with you to pick this dream of earning a doctoral degree and walk through it together?

Yes, that's great.

Olive

We met with Olive at her home and enjoyed sitting on her cosy red leather sofas. She read one of the first draft versions of this chapter and then we started our conversation:

1. Hi Olive. Please tell us a bit about your dreams.

   There are a few big things I've dreamt about for some time:

   - *First, I dream of having a new job, rather than the one I have today – multimedia coordinator for the websites owned by a media group. This is both a dream and a necessity for me, as I need to make this change if I am to have a more balanced life, with more time to focus on my other dreams, my hobbies and social life. I would like to work outside the world of mass media, being more of a strategist and manager than the one fighting in the trenches, always covering the latest "breaking news", or handling the many crises and problems that show up every day in this line of work.*

   - *The second, and the one dearest to me, is the dream of becoming a bar singer. A few days ago I started taking canto lessons. I enjoy this a lot and, the more I think about it and also work on my lessons, the more I can see myself doing this.*

   - *A third but more distant dream is to open my own coffee bar, where I can manifest my passion for singing, creating an intimate atmosphere for people with coffee and good taste. However, I realize it is way too soon for me to work on this dream as I don't have the necessary financials, nor a favourable context to start working on it on the short term.*

2. If you were to choose one and apply the model we propose in this book, which would it be?

I think this choice is easy – the dream of being a bar singer. Ever since I was a child, I have been passionate about music. For a while I took piano lessons which I really enjoyed. Unfortunately for me, my teacher had to move and left the town where I lived. Since she was the only piano teacher in town, I couldn't resume my lessons, so I stopped working on it altogether. Next, in high school I bought a classical guitar and I learned how to play it by myself. Whenever I got together with my friends, and occasionally at parties with people my age, I used to accompany others and sing along.

Now that I am an adult, one of my hobbies is to go to karaoke bars and sing with others. Not long ago, one lucky evening, I was surprised by a canto teacher who heard me sing a few songs. She told me that I have what it takes to be a good singer and that she is willing to help me, for free.

Since then, every other week, I meet with her for rehearsals and lessons on how to breathe, diction and how to improve my voice.

3. This is a good story. If you were to envision yourself being a bar singer, how would it be?

I do not dream of being a famous singer, with albums and videos published on TV. I simply want to sing solo or with a band, in a cosy bar where people go to relax, enjoy themselves and listen to music. I want to make people feel good while they listen to my singing, have them relax and disconnect from the stress of day to day living. I dream of having a small but regular audience, coming to hear me sing every other week, simply because they enjoy my music and I enjoy sharing my music with them. I don't see myself doing this for lots of money, but for the human connection side of it.

Anna and Amelia

We met Anna and Amelia in Amelia's town house on the south coast in the UK. Their dream is different from the others in this book – they both have already had successful careers, but now they want to set up a business together. So, this is how two people can jointly achieve a dream.

They are in the process of founding a design company. When we met them, they had just finished a discussion about an upcoming trade show that they will be attending. This will be the first real event in their new business – and it's a great time for them to reflect on their dream.

1. So, tell us about your dream . . .

    Anna: *Well I think a lot of our dream is subconscious. We did not explicitly say it all out loud but just naturally started working together. We have balancing skills, but we have not said to each other "this is how I see the future. This is my dream". I suspect that to some extent we have different dreams.*

    Amelia: *Yes that's true. But there is one thing we are both clear on – this is a dream with a very practical aspect, in that it is about making money. But not just making money in any way we can, it is about making money from a product that we are passionate about. That is a product that is developed from original creative insights, a high level of design, and exhibits high quality production.*

2. Then your dream is all about making a product for sale – an original and high quality product, but a product nevertheless?

    Anna: *Not exactly. Although we are starting with some products, it's less about these specific products – the dream is about us building a brand which is recognized* *for a certain level and style of design. In our dream, as the brand becomes recognized, we would happily be an outlet for other individual designers and artists who share our values and outlook.*

Amelia: *The brand is something we want to feel passionate and excited about. As an artist I have to feel that I can happily associate our designs with our brand. But as I said before, the dream has a very practical angle as well. Let me explain an important aspect for me. I will be retiring from my main occupation soon and my dream is that this business will at least provide me with money to bridge the gap between my pension income and my salary now. If we achieve that, then I will regard that as the first major step in a successful business.*

Anna: *But there are no constraints on what we are aiming for. We will see how it goes, and we will push this to be as successful as we can, whilst remaining true to our vision of the brand.*

3. So then, this is more about business than personal fulfilment?

Anna: *Again no, it's not that simple. We want a successful business, but it is important to both of us that the business is delivering something we really believe in. So, whilst having a successful business is critically important, if that is all we do, then it will not be our dream.*

Amelia: *The business has to be something I enjoy. Even if our first products are not as successful as we expect, I want to get something out of going through the process of running a business. We will learn, and we will have fun. At times we will be stretched, but that's all part of the enjoyment. Right now, we are investing in a stand at a trade show. This is a big investment for a business the size of ours, but it feels right – because, apart from anything else,* *it will force us to learn. So you could say that part of the dream is to learn more, to keep on progressing the dream further and further.*

Anna: *We have already learnt a lot already just by starting to talk to people about our business idea. We've had some great advice already – and we've already had our fingers burnt with suppliers who have not delivered, or have delivered late. But, that's all part of the fun and learning!*

4.   So, can we be clear what the business will do?

Anna: *To be precise – we are planning to start a business making and selling handmade cards. These cards will be made on high quality paper and hand embossed based on Amelia's designs. They will be offered for sale at Christmas and other holidays and throughout the year. Additionally, we will offer a bespoke service for weddings and other times when people want personalized cards. The cards will be the same quality as a small piece of art. We expect to sell them online and in art galleries. Once we have done this, we plan to expand into making prints as pictures to be hung on walls, using similar designs and similar manufacturing processes. From that – who knows? We don't know where the business will end, but we have a very clear product to start out with.*

5.   It sounds great. Is there anything you would like to add?

Amelia: *One thing I want to add is that the way our business unfolds, or how we go about achieving our dream, will be driven by our experience as designers. Designers and artists don't learn by just thinking – we learn by doing – that is by actually designing and creating art. So, part of the dream is about giving us a situation in which we can do more and do different things to really drive our creative energies.*

Questions to Ask Yourself

- Am I conscious of all the good things I dream about on a regular basis?
- Have I selected just one important dream to choose to make a reality?
- What is the outcome I want to achieve?
- Can I *really* imagine that outcome clearly?
- Can I explain my dream to others in a way that they can understand it?

Summary

All of the most successful people started out with a dream. To share their success you need to identify the dreams that are most important to you. Go through and list the dreams that really matter to you. To make your dreaming achievable, you should focus on one dream at a time and spend time making it as clear and specific as you can – so select one of the dreams that is most important to you. Try to get to the point where you have a vision of what it will be like to achieve this dream that you believe in and are excited by.

2   THINK

> *A man is but the product of his thoughts. What he thinks, he becomes.*
>
> Mahatma Gandhi

The Goal

You have a dream. You know where you want to get to. The next question is obvious: how are you going to get there? This chapter is about thinking through the route to your dream. It works hand-in-hand with the following chapter which is about drawing your own map.

Once you have become excited about your dream, it can be really tempting to rush ahead straightaway and try and achieve it. We are going to suggest something different. We are going to ask you to *sit still* and *think*. We don't want you to lose your energy and enthusiasm for your dream, but our experience has taught us that the people who achieve the most *think* about how to achieve things and have a way to achieve them. Thinking need not take long, but it is always valuable.

The Map

Throughout this chapter we will show you how to break down the big challenge of achieving your dream by using the image of a map. A map shows the way to get somewhere – in this case it shows the way to achieve your dream. Your own map will be specific and unique for you and your dream. What the map looks like and how you draw it, we will discuss in the next chapter. Don't worry about this for now. Just start thinking.

Thinking is especially important when it comes to realizing dreams. When you have done something many times you know how to do it again. You have developed memories and routines which show you the way. But with dreams, at least the most exciting and worthwhile ones, you have not done it before. You have to build a map from scratch.

A good map will help you get to where you want to go, but only if you know where you want to get to! If your dream is too vague, your map will be imprecise and hard to follow. As you start to think about your map, ensure that your dream is clear. Don't worry if your dream is not perfectly clear – Thinking and Drawing will naturally clarify your dream. But if it is very unclear, go back to Chapter 1 and do some more dreaming first.

When you develop your own map, there are four main things to think about:

- The things that need to be done to achieve your dream.
- The order you need to do them in.
- The way you will get them done.
- What you need to get them done.

The main idea behind building a map is to break the big challenge of achieving your dream into small steps. Each step should be the sort of activity you understand and can do. If you don't understand an activity, you need to break it down into more detail until you do. Don't worry at this stage whether you have the time, ability or resources to do the steps. The key thing for now is to work out what they are.

Once you know the things you need to do to achieve your dream, you must structure them into the order you need to get them done. There is a logical sequence to most activities. We will explore in the next chapter how you can do this to create a really effective map.

Beyond that, you need to think about how you will get the steps done and what other things you need to get them done. Can you do everything yourself, or do you need help? Do you need any tools or resources?

A Map that Works

Building a good map can be a real challenge, but it is important to create one. Once you have built your own map, you are a long way forward into making your dream come true. A dream without a map is just a dream, once you have a good map it is a realizable goal.

A map may require you to do demanding things, but it must be based in reality. The map must be workable. We can all do more than we realize, but building a map is the time when you switch from abstract dreaming to planting your feet firmly on the ground.

One thing to always remember when building your map, and later on when you are following it: you don't have to do this alone. There will be lots of people willing and able to help you.

Things to Think about: Your Map's Elements

The essence of map making is breaking the giant goal that is your dream into smaller steps. Each individual step may be very small, but each step takes you a little way towards achieving your dream. Even the best things happen one step at a time.

Start by thinking about all the things you need to do to achieve your dream. We often find it handy to keep lists of all the things we think we may need to do. Write the activities down as a list, picture or any other way you keep track of ideas. Don't worry about the structure or order of these lists. Keep them in any format you like, as long as it is meaningful to you.

Get in the habit of keeping such lists. As you go through your daily routine, you will find yourself thinking of things to add that you need to do to achieve your dream.

Your dream is personal to you, and what you need to do to achieve it will be unique. Your map will contain the activities that only your dream needs to be realized. We cannot give you an off-the-shelf list for your map, but we can give you an approach and some questions to think about, to get you thinking in the right way:

1. Start at the highest level and work downwards into the detail:
   - What must be in place for my dream to be reality?
   - So, what steps do I need to take, to put these things in place?
   - Then, how should I go about taking these steps?
2. Then start to think about the help, tools and resources you need to work through the tasks on your map:
   - What do I deliver by myself?
   - Who do I need help from to get things done? Is there anyone I can share the work with? There are lots of people who will be willing to help.
   - What do I need to make, borrow or buy to get things done?
   - What money or other resources do I need? How can I get hold of this?
3. Next think about the sequence of activities:
   - Which order should I do the activities in? Can some things only be done once others have?
   - How long will the sequence of activities take?
   - How much time do I have? If it is less than my activities – how can I streamline the work to fit the time I have available?

4. Finally think about all the unknowns and potential problems you could encounter on the way. You should not become obsessed by things that can go wrong. But you should be aware that plans very rarely happen exactly as you expect. To avoid being put off by every or any problem that arises, you should plan for them:

    - What is most likely to go wrong – and what can I do to avoid this?
    - What would increase my chances of success?

How will I Know I've Done Well?

The purpose of Thinking is to get ready for Drawing, which we will explain in the next chapter. To some extent you won't know if you've done your thinking well until you try and draw. But there is some general guidance we can give at this stage. The indications that you are doing your thinking well are:

- **You know how you will start to achieve your dream.** To go on a journey you have to know where to start!
- **You have thought about the things you do not yet know or understand.** To achieve most dreams you have to be prepared to do some analysis, exploration, experimentation or research. How will you get this done?
- **Your thinking is really about achieving *your* dream.** Sometimes in thinking we can lose sight of our

goal and start thinking about all sorts of other interesting things. Achieving dreams takes focus! Park those other ideas and dreams for now. You can come back to them when your dream is achieved.

- **You are not trying to solve every problem or work out every detail now.** If you try and make absolutely everything clear, you will spend forever thinking and never get on to doing. We believe the Think stage is critically important, but we also know it can be a trap where you spend forever refining your map.

- **You are doing _real_ thinking.** How long you should spend thinking depends on how big and complex your dream is, and how effective your thinking is. Thinking can be done in a few hours or a few days of proper effort. If you are spending more time than that, then you are probably over doing it. But we mean a few hours or days of real thinking, not it being in the back of your mind for a few days!

What Our Heroes Say

Alex

We meet Alex in the student canteen, it is busy and noisy, but we manage to find a table. We have a conversation to help him think about how he will get a doctoral degree.

1. What must be in place for my dream to be reality?

    Quite a few elements:
    *   *First, I need to pick a specific medical field in which to get specialized and certified.*
    *   *Identify a good topic for writing a research thesis, which will earn me the certification I dream of having.*
    *   *Establish a research team and obtain the resources I need to work on my research thesis.*
    *   *Acquire new research skills.*
    *   *Do the research.*
    *   *Write the research thesis.*
    *   *Present my thesis and "defend" it in front of an official evaluation committee.*

2. So, what steps do I need to take, to put these things in place?

    *   *Pick the medical field – I want my research to be closely related to my job as a doctor. That's why I want to find a medical speciality that will allow me to also do research. The steps I need to go through are: think and decide on a field that suits me, study and take*

the standard exam in that field, so that I am allowed to work on my research thesis.

- *Identify a topic for my research thesis – I need to read medical research literature on the topics that interest me, identify the latest trends in research, formulate an interesting working hypothesis to investigate.*
- *Establish a research team alongside which to do the research – this is important because I need both an experienced guide with whom to collaborate, exchange ideas and troubleshoot results, but also because there are so many tasks to manage, that working in a team is essential in order to succeed. This element would require the following steps:*
  - *Find a senior investigator to sponsor the research and coach me and my team.*
  - *Find a team to start the research with.*
- *Obtain the resources I need – there are plenty of steps to go through:*
  - *Write a grant proposal.*
  - *Evaluate and document the resources I will need to conduct the research.*
  - *Submit the required documentation to the national grant funding committee.*
  - *Get the approval and the resources from the committee.*
- *Acquire new research skills:*
  - *Participate in other similar projects.*
  - *Go to classes and workshops that share useful tips for young researchers.*
- *Doing the research – this is again pretty complex:*
  - *Write a research plan.*
  - *Execute the research plan.*
  - *Document research findings.*

- *Troubleshoot research problems.*
- *Analyze all research data.*

- *Write the research thesis – this involves fewer steps: aggregate all research and literature data, correlate all findings and conclusions, write the thesis itself and make a good presentation.*
- *Present my thesis to an official evaluation committee – there are a few very important steps: schedule the evaluation meeting, prepare for possible questions they could ask, do the "defending" itself and get the degree I want in the medical research field I've chosen.*

3. Then, how should I go about taking these steps?

   When doing the research, I must use standardized research methods (officially recognized by the medical community), the results must be verified using at least two approved methods and confirmed by both, and the presentation and documentation I create must follow the rigid standards imposed by the research community.

4. What do I deliver by myself?

   Even though I will get lots of help from others, I will be involved in every step. Only during the research itself will there be things researched individually by each team member. I will need to get involved only in reading and evaluating the results and conclusions.

5. Who do I need help from to get things done? Is there anyone I can share the work with?

   I will need help from lots of people. First I must find a senior investigator to sponsor the research. With his/her help, I will need to find a research team and get the approvals I need to start the research. The research team will be vital to finish things up and to get the final certification. I will also need additional help from people in my network, to make sure I present the best research thesis I possibly can.

6. What do I need to make, borrow or buy to get things done?

That's a very good question. I know I will need plenty of things but, at this moment, I can't really evaluate them. I need to start working on this dream and while working on my grant proposal I can evaluate what I need in a realistic way.

7. What money or other resources do I need? How can I get hold of this?

Again, I cannot evaluate this at this moment. All I know is that the resources I will need to conduct my research and write the thesis with will be received via the grant funding committee we are applying to.

8. Which order should I do the activities in? Can some things only be done once others have?

Most of them are done in the order I've shared them. There are a few things that can be done in parallel though, such as finding the topic for the research thesis and establishing the research team. Also, my work on acquiring new research skills can be done in parallel with any of the other elements involved in this dream. It is simply a matter of taking advantage of any learning opportunities that come up as I go along.

9. How long will the sequence of activities take? Let's take the big elements one by one:

- *Pick a specific medical field in which to get specialized and certified – 1 month.*
- *Identify a good topic for writing a research thesis – 1 month.*
- *Establish a research team – 1 month.*
- *Obtain the resources I need to work on my research and the thesis – 2 months.*
- *Acquire new research skills – I don't have a specific time estimation for this.*
- *Do the research – 7 months.*
- *Write the research thesis – 2 to 3 weeks.*
- *Present my thesis and "defend" it in front of an official evaluation committee – 2 weeks.*

10. How much time do I have? If it is less than my activities, how can I streamline the work to fit the time I have available?

    I do not have a deadline imposed by the medical community. I can even do this in 2 years. However, considering what I want to do after this dream is accomplished, I should finish in a maximum of 1.5 years. The optimal time for me to finish this dream in would be 1 year.

11. What is most likely to go wrong – and what can I do to avoid this? There are quite a few things that can make it harder to be successful:

- *The grant funding committee does not approve the research thesis and resources needed for it. I will need to be extra careful about this and make the best supporting documentation I can. Also, it will help if I manage to find a senior investigator to sponsor my research who is well known and influential in the medical research community. Even if this fails, I can explore additional funding options – like getting a private investor interested in funding our research.*

- *The working hypothesis I will make for my research thesis and grant proposal could be wrong. To avoid this mistake I should do as much documentation as possible before creating it. Also, the thesis should be created based on preliminary research that I have done so far and then be validated by an experienced researcher.*

- *The evaluation committee does not agree with the conclusions of my research thesis which means I will not receive the certification. Here, I should be careful when centralizing the research results and writing the paper. If any conclusion feels debatable, I will allow more time to improve some aspects of the research and redo certain experiments in a better way.*

12.　What would increase my chances of success? There are two things that will really boost my chances of success:

- *The first is to find a research topic I am passionate about. Something that gets my mind working and makes both me and the research team feel excited to work on.*

- *It would be of tremendous help to find a supervisor with experience and a good reputation in the medical research community, who is able to guide me and the team when things get complicated and help in getting the approvals and resources needed for carrying out the research.*

Olive

It's now Olive's turn to think about how she can turn her dream of becoming a bar singer into reality.

1. What must be in place for my dream to be reality?

   There are four big elements:
   - *Improve my voice and singing technique.*
   - *Learn how to work with the equipment used on most stages.*
   - *Find places and contexts where I can sing and experiment.*
   - *Find a bar where I can do professional singing and sign a contract with them.*

2. So, what steps do I need to take, to put these things in place?

   Let's take each element one by one:
   - *Improve my voice and singing technique – find a teacher/coach (which I already have), practise regularly, experiment with various musical genres, choose the musical genre(s) I am best at.*
   - *Learn how to work with the equipment used on most stages – find a few places (karaoke bars, rehearsal halls, etc.) where I can work with such equipment for free, find someone to show me the ropes when needed.*
   - *Find places and contexts where I can sing and experiment – find bars and/or musical groups where people regularly meet and sing, find a cover band to occasionally sing with.*
   - *Find a bar where I can do professional singing and sign a contract with them – identify bars which hire singers and bands to perform on a regular basis,*

create a demo, and apply for a job with the bars I find or join a group which already has a contract.

3. Then, how should I go about taking these steps?

   There is nothing specific about how I should take these steps. I simply need to be disciplined and keep working at it.

4. What do I deliver by myself?

   Everything needs to be done by me. Others have a role to play only in a few of the steps but I should always be the one doing things, starting discussions, asking for help, etc.

5. Who do I need help from to get things done? Is there anyone I can share the work with?

   I do need help from others on improving my voice and singing technique (e.g. my canto teacher, friends and other people passionate about singing) and to learn how to work with the equipment used on stages (e.g. help from friends working in this area). To find a place where I can sing and experiment, I might need some help from friends as well.

6. What do I need to make, borrow or buy to get things done?

   This is easy as I need very little and I plan to do this as cost effectively as possible. The only thing I need to buy for sure is my own microphone and use it to record myself or when singing on a stage.

7. What money or other resources do I need? How can I get hold of this?

    I need around 20 dollars to buy a reasonably good microphone to get me started. I will also need some money to go out, in karaoke bars and other places where people go out to sing. This is nothing extra from what I spend now when going out during my free time.

8. Which order should I do the activities in? Can some things only be done once others have?

    From all the big elements, I can start in parallel on improving my voice and singing technique and finding places where I can sing and experiment regularly. Then, I think it would be good to learn how to work with the equipment used on most stages. Last is the step of finding a bar where to sing and sign a contract.

9. How long will the sequence of activities take?

    Each of the big elements that make up my dream should take a few months each. The biggest time consumers will be improving my voice and singing technique and finding places to sing and experiment. I think I need to work on them in parallel for at least 5 to 6 months.

    Learning how to work with the equipment used on most stages should not take me more than two months. Finding a bar and signing a contract – this is very hard to estimate. I really don't know how long it will take me. Also, it's important for me to get into the position where I am good enough to have a chance of being hired.

10. How much time do I have? If it is less than my activities – how can I streamline the work to fit the time I have available?

I do not have a deadline and I can allow for this dream as much time as I need. Key for me is to keep regularly working on this and not have big breaks between rehearsals and working on improving my voice. Not more than two weeks anyway. I would like to achieve this dream in one to two years.

11. What is most likely to go wrong – and what can I do to avoid this?

There are not that many things that can go wrong. I can identify only a few:
- *If the current collaboration with my canto teacher (helping me for free) is no longer possible, I will need to pay for a few additional lessons. Also, if I really can't find free rehearsal hall(s) I will need to occasionally rent one. This shouldn't require me to make huge investments and I should be able to pay for them from my monthly salary.*
- *Other perils would be for me to get sick or catch a nasty cold, which would stop me singing and rehearsing for a while. However, there's nothing special I can really do about that.*

12. What would increase my chances of success?

There are two things I can think about:
- *Quit smoking – even though it would help with my voice, I am not willing to give it up. It is something I enjoy. The only thing I can bring myself to do is to smoke a bit less.*

- *Get constant feedback. I think it would be great to record as many rehearsals as possible, share them with my canto teacher and get feedback from her, even for rehearsals that are not done in her presence. Also getting feedback from other people who are passionate and knowledgeable about music would help.*

Anna and Amelia

It was a wet and windy day when we met Anna and Amelia – so we had to dash into a nearby cafe to have our discussion about their design business.

1.   What must be in place for our dream to be reality?

     There are really three main elements we need to get right:

     - *Get the product ready to send when we get an order, and more quickly some minimum stock to support marketing.*
     - *Be clear how we will sell, and at what price – both to a retail and wholesale market.*
     - *Work through the process of production to ensure there are no hidden problems in making our product.*

2.   So, what steps do we need to take, to put these things in place?

     - *Finalize the design of the products. Amelia has made a variety of samples but we need to agree which ones we will actually start making and marketing.*
     - *We need to finalize the way we will make them – we have produced very small volumes to date. This will be fine to start with, but if we get big orders we will need to think how to manage this.*
     - *We need some samples to show potential clients, and then we will need some product ready to fulfil orders as they come in.*
     - *We need to get some clarity over the price. This is a high end handmade card and to cover the cost of the*

time used the price is quite high for an ordinary card, but if it is seen as a piece of art (as it should be) then the price is really reasonable. But we have no experience of setting prices.

- *We need some way of marketing and selling – at the very least this could be a website, but we may use other channels such as trade shows.*
- *There are lots of business admin things to set up (bank account, invoices, database of customers), finishing touches to the products (envelopes, packaging materials and so on), and simple practical things such as where to keep the stock and how to transfer it from Amelia to Anna as we live far apart.*

3. Then, how should we go about taking these steps?

- *The most important thing is that we are clear about who does what. Some roles are interchangeable, but some are not. Basically, Amelia is the main designer and producer and Anna does everything else. But even this is too simple – we have not done anything like this before, so almost certainly there are loads of things we have not thought of that we will have to find out as we go along. So we have to be responsive. We live far apart so we will talk often to check progress and help each other out – whilst we have different roles we really want this to be a true partnership.*

4. What do we deliver by ourselves?

Most things need to be done by ourselves – we don't employ or work with anyone else!

5. Who do we need help from to get things done? Is there anyone we can share the work with?

    - *Well, we are lucky in that we are doing this together. We have complementary skills, but we also have a shared dream. This means we are never alone; there is always someone to talk to about things. If we ever feel stuck, instead of banging our heads against the wall we can talk and the other one can take over.*

    - *However we do call on others. Amelia has used her contacts for advice, particularly one friend Jonathan who set up a business a couple of years ago and is very helpful. Amelia also has the contact details of other artists and designers who have done related things to get their ideas and advice. Plus Anna's husband has lots of business experience – he knows nothing about design, but he can help us thinking about marketing, finance and so on. Otherwise we ask anyone and everyone we know for opinions and advice.*

6. What money or other resources do we need? How can we get hold of this?

    - *By the normal standards of setting up a business, we don't need lots of money – there are no premises or employees and we don't pay ourselves, but we do need some. We have put some money each into the business, but we also have a friend who has given us a line of credit we can call on, for the next year or so, until we start making money. I should stress this really is not a lot of money, but it makes it easier.*

    - *I (Amelia) think it really helps that I am working. I don't currently need the business to be profitable and this takes the pressure off and allows me to be fully crea-*

tive. If we need to stop and take time to think about something, we can.

7. Which order should we do the activities in? Can some things only be done once others have?

   For many of the tasks, the order does not matter that much, but there are some big chunks we need to do first. The most important thing is to agree who does what, then get the basic product and price right, then work on our sales channels.

8. How long will the sequence of activities take?

   Fortunately, we are not dependent on income from the business, though we would love to be in that position of course. So at the moment, the tasks will take as long as they need to. But in terms of our targets, we aim to be up and running at some level in a few months. Although it may take a year or more to become profitable!

9. How much time do we have? If it is less than our activities – how can we streamline the work to fit the time we have available?

   - *We both have other jobs. Amelia is a full time teacher and Anna is a part time medical herbalist. The work has to fit around the other things we do. Also there will always be interruptions, we both have elderly relatives who needed looking after and that has slowed us down already – but that's just the real world. We think we have enough time, and if the business takes off, we will make more time!*
   - *Designing and making this product takes whatever time it takes. Of course, it cannot take forever, there is a commercial reality. But the creative process is not*

something you can force into a fixed period of time. Sometimes it is very quick, and on other occasions very long. We are making unique handmade objects and we must allow ourselves the freedom to develop them in whatever time it takes.

10. What is most likely to go wrong – and what can we do to avoid this?

- *We are optimistic that we have a really nice product and it will sell, but there two things we worry about. Firstly, as neither of us has done anything like this before, we really worry about whether we have missed something out. Secondly, we worry that we may get the price wrong, but this has to be an expensive product as it is handmade and that takes real time.*
- *One thing that is important is the whole quality of the produce – including all the details. The cards are beautiful so we have to find packaging and labelling that are of a similar quality, otherwise the product will be undermined.*

11. What would increase our chances of success?

- *Good, experienced friends willing to give us advice.*
- *Testing and willingness to refine the products depending on the response from customers. We are willing to change everything. The designs we have are today's product. It is a luxury product and we will change it over time.*
- *Treating this as a real priority and not letting other things get in the way.*
- *A bit of luck!*

Questions to Ask Yourself

- Are you sufficiently clear about the big elements that need to go into your map?
- What is the very first thing you are going to do to achieve your dream? What is the second thing you will do?
- Do you have a vision of the order of steps in your map?
- Who are you going to ask for support in following your dream?
- What other resources do you need, and how will you get hold of them?
- Is there anything that is likely to go wrong?
- Is there anything that would help increase your chances of success?

Summary

In this chapter we asked you to think more about your dream, and introduced the concept of a map. The map will be your personal guide to achieving your dream, but first you must create it. The idea behind maps is simple – break the big goal of achieving your dream into a set of much smaller, achievable steps. Creating a good map starts with thinking through all the things that need to be done to achieve your dream, the order in which they should be done, how you will do them, as well as what help and support you will need along the way.

3 DRAW

Drawing is putting a line (a)round an idea.

Henri Matisse

The Goal

In our previous chapter we really asked you a lot of questions. This was not to paralyze you or to stop you from working on making your dream come true, but to ensure you put enough thought into what you need to do.

However, doing a bit of thinking is rarely enough, especially when you are new to the habit of tackling your life's biggest dreams. There's one more important step you need to take before you start working on your dream: drawing your own map. By drawing we mean creating a visual image of your dream and how to achieve it.

Drawing is something few people do once they grow from children to adults, yet it is such a powerful exercise. In this chapter we will encourage you to draw and help you to learn how to do it in a way that is both natural and helpful. At the end of this drawing exercise, you should be able to visualize the path to making your dream come true in a way you have not been able to so far.

Why Draw?

There are many reasons for you to draw your own map. The first and most important is that it gives a true feel for the adventure you are about to embark on. Most of the time we believe it is enough to think about our dreams now and again. But we don't realize that thinking alone never gives us a complete or fully structured overview of what we really need to do.

Drawing all the elements, showing how you are going to make the dream come true, pushes you to think more deeply about what you need to do. It also helps you visualize the dream in its entirety and complexity. This exercise will always create a cascade of ideas and will help reveal things you have not thought about, possible problems or actions you could take to increase your chances of success. It will also enable you to come up with new ideas and new approaches. Drawing really helps you focus and visualize the journey towards making your dream come true.

Another important benefit is that the map can be a great tool for communicating your dream to others when explaining what you intend to do, particularly when you need other people's help. Showing a visual map to people helps them understand faster what they need to do to help you out. It also helps them point out elements you have missed in your thinking.

A less appreciated reason for drawing your own map, and keeping it updated, is that it helps you become more disciplined in accomplishing your dream. It will stop you from lying to yourself about the real progress you are making. You've drawn your path to making the dream come true – you know where you should be in your journey at almost any time and you won't be able to fool yourself that you are halfway there when you have not even started. On the positive side, it also helps you get a feeling of progress. You can put it in front of you and understand how well or how badly you are doing.

Also, when you get to the end of your dream and you've made it happen, you can visualize your trip from the starting point to the end. You will easily recall all the things you have learned, all the adjustments you've made on the way and apply your newly acquired knowledge when making the map of your next dream.

How to Draw

Drawing is a very personal activity and is done in various ways by different people. We don't want to impose one way of drawing your map over another, as there is no right or wrong way of doing it. We simply want to share a few principles, tools and examples that can be used to get you started with your map drawing. Don't worry if you are initially putting down crazy or half thought through ideas, words which mean something only to you and nothing to someone else. This is first about your thinking and what works best for you. Only later on can it be used as a presentation for other people, if you feel comfortable about it.

While learning and applying the concepts we are sharing, it is important for you to develop and improve your own style, in a way that feels natural to you, based on what you observe and what you learn.

Now . . . where do you start?

Take a blank sheet of paper and place it in front of you, preferably in landscape orientation. In the centre, write the name of your dream or draw a symbol of it, whichever you prefer. That was easy, wasn't it? Now, let's go to the hard part – all those questions we asked you to think about. You need to draw the elements that make up the answers to those questions and include them in your map. You don't have to draw absolutely everything, just the elements that make sense for the questions relevant to your dream.

Let's see how this works, for each set of questions we recommended during the Thinking stage, using our dream of publishing this book. As we do this, we will show the example of how our drawing for this book grew. At the end of the chapter we'll show the maps created by each of our heroes. Looking at these drawings will make our words much clearer.

1. The big elements that make up the dream – we asked you to think about the answers to the following questions:
    a) What must be in place for my dream to be reality?
    b) So, what steps do I need to take, to put these things in place?
    c) Then, how should I go about taking these steps?
    - For each of the elements that need to be in place for your dream to become a reality, draw a separate box with its name inside.
    - Make sure you have some space between elements, to add more details later on.
    - For each of these elements, write down the answers to the second question, each in its own separate little box.
    - For any of these steps, if there is anything specific you want to do, make sure you put it in a small separate box.
    - Now connect each step to its appropriate element and then all the elements to the dream, with a simple line (straight or curved, it doesn't matter).
    - You should now have a visual representation that looks similar to a spider's web.

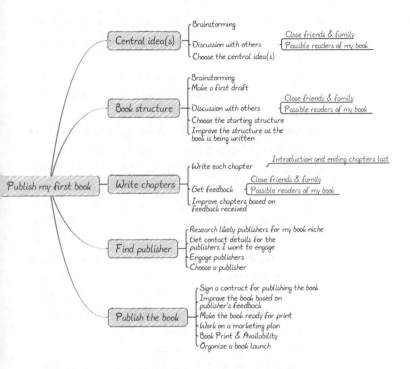

2. Who and what you need to achieve your dream – we asked you to think on the following questions:

a) What do I deliver by myself?

b) Who do I need help from to get things done? Is there anyone I can share the work with?

c) What do I need to make, borrow or buy to get things done?

d) What money or other resources do I need? How can I get hold of this?

- For the things you want to deliver on your own, there's no need to draw anything else.

- If a step is on your map, without anyone else's name associated with it, you must assume you need to do it.
- If it helps, you can draw a symbol near each step to use as a visual reminder that you are responsible for it.
- Make sure you use the same symbol everywhere so that you don't confuse yourself later on.
- Make sure you identify the people whose help you need to get things done. Make a separate box called "people", "helpers" or anything else that suggests this idea and then mention the people you need, each in a separate box connected to the first. Now connect the "people" box to the dream. Think where these people need to contribute and draw a symbol for each step where you need their help. You can also write their name near the name of the step where they will help.
- For c) and d) (if they apply to your dream), draw separate boxes for the things you need to make, borrow or buy and the money you need. Think of this as a "parent", where each "parent" describes a category of things you need. Then, each of the items within this "parent" category should have their own little box, connected to its parent. For example, if you need to buy some photographic equipment for your dream of becoming a professional photographer, create a box called "Buy equipment" and then other boxes for the "camera", "tripod", "lens" and everything else that needs to be bought, each connected with a line to the "Buy equipment" box. Then connect "Buy equipment" to your dream, with another line.

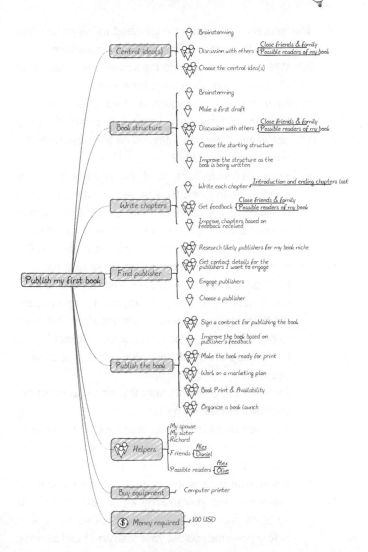

Publish my first book

- **Central idea(s)**
  - Brainstorming
  - Discussion with others — Close friends & family / Possible readers of my book
  - Choose the central idea(s)

- **Book structure**
  - Brainstorming
  - Make a first draft
  - Discussion with others — Close friends & family / Possible readers of my book
  - Choose the starting structure
  - Improve the structure as the book is being written

- **Write chapters**
  - Write each chapter — Introduction and ending chapters last
  - Get feedback — Close friends & family / Possible readers of my book
  - Improve chapters based on feedback received

- **Find publisher**
  - Research likely publishers for my book niche
  - Get contact details for the publishers I want to engage
  - Engage publishers
  - Choose a publisher

- **Publish the book**
  - Sign a contract for publishing the book
  - Improve the book based on publisher's feedback
  - Make the book ready for print
  - Work on a marketing plan
  - Book Print & Availability
  - Organize a book launch

- **Helpers**
  - My spouse
  - My sister
  - Richard
  - Friends — Alex / Daniel
  - Possible readers — Alex / Olive

- **Buy equipment** — Computer printer

- **($) Money required** — 100 USD

3. The sequence in which things need to be done – we asked you to ponder on the following questions:

a) Which order should I do the activities in? Can some things only be done once others have?

b) How long will the sequence of activities take?

c) How much time do I have? If it is less than my activities – how can I streamline the work to fit the time I have available?

- For question a), look at all the big elements that need to be in place to achieve your dream. Add a number by the name of each element to indicate the order you think they need to be completed in. If some elements can be worked in parallel, it is OK to use the same order number for all of them.

- For question c), look at each element and all the steps needed to make it happen. Try to evaluate the time you, or the people who help you, will need to get it done. It doesn't have to be an exact figure; just a rough idea of how much time you think is needed.

- For each big element, write the time you estimate, somewhere near its name.

- Now add up the time you need for all the elements to get a rough approximation of how much time you will need to make the dream come true.

- If this total time is longer than the time you have available, then you already know you will have a problem and where. You will be able to view it before you start, adjust your map and build a better one.

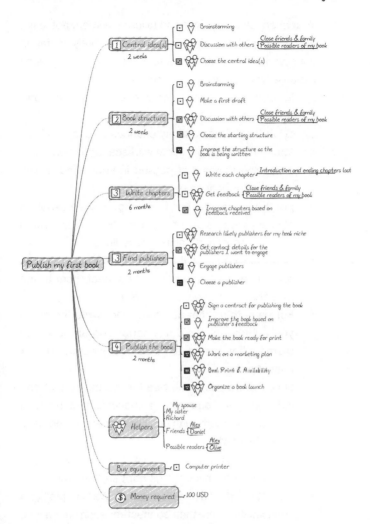

Publish my first book

1 Central idea(s) — 2 weeks
- Brainstorming
- Discussion with others — Close friends & family / Possible readers of my book
- Choose the central idea(s)

2 Book structure — 2 weeks
- Brainstorming
- Make a first draft
- Discussion with others — Close friends & family / Possible readers of my book
- Choose the starting structure
- Improve the structure as the book is being written

3 Write chapters — 6 months
- Write each chapter — Introduction and ending chapters last
- Get feedback — Close friends & family / Possible readers of my book
- Improve chapters based on feedback received

3 Find publisher — 2 months
- Research likely publishers for my book niche
- Get contact details for the publishers I want to engage
- Engage publishers
- Choose a publisher

4 Publish the book — 2 months
- Sign a contract for publishing the book
- Improve the book based on publisher's feedback
- Make the book ready for print
- Work on a marketing plan
- Book Print & Availability
- Organize a book launch

Helpers
- My spouse
- My sister
- Richard
- Friends — Alex / Daniel
- Possible readers — Alex / Olive

Buy equipment
- Computer printer

Money required
- 100 USD

4. Your chances of success and failure – last but not least, we asked you to think about what is likely to fail in your work on making the dream happen and what can increase your chances of success:

   a) What is most likely to go wrong – and what can I do to avoid this?

   b) What would increase my chances of success?

   - You don't need to think of wild scenarios here, only about the things that pop-up in your head, which have a real chance of happening.

   - For the things that can go wrong, make a separate element with its own box called "Risks" or "Watch outs" or something along those lines.

   - Write the name of the things that can go wrong, each in its own little box and connect them to the parent element you just created.

   - For each thing that can go wrong, write the steps you will take to avoid this happening and connect them to their parent, as you did for step one in your map drawing.

   - Now do the same exercise for the things that can increase your chances of success: first make a section for them with an appropriate name (e.g. "Possibilities").

   - List each thing that can help and, for each, what you will do to make things happen that way.

   - Make sure the two big boxes for "Watch outs" and "Possibilities" are then connected, each with a line, to your dream.

Publish my first book

⚠ Watchouts

- Create a weak book structure
  - Talk with an experienced author - Richard
- Write some poor chapters
  - Get feedback from an experienced author - Richard
- Not able find a publisher
  - Get contacts from Richard
  - Talk with friends about people they know working in the publishing business

Possibilities

- Research early for book publisher contacts
  - Get in touch with a publisher and talk about the book + ask for feedback

This is one big map, isn't it?

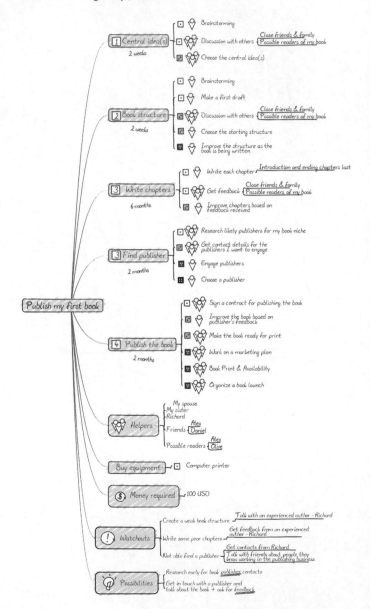

Well, that's great. The map will show in a visual way the work you need to do to make things happen. But how should you go about creating it? What are the tools you can use for this task?

The Tools for Drawing

You probably won't be surprised when we tell you that almost anything you can draw on will do. The tools are not important, the exercise of drawing and thinking is. You should pick something that you can imagine yourself using, a tool you are comfortable with and one where you don't need to spend time learning how to use it. Here are some tools we know work great for drawing maps of your dreams:

- **Pen and paper** – one of the most productive way of drawing your map is to take a few pieces of paper (A3 or A4, the bigger the better), a pen and start drawing.
- **Whiteboards** – they work well, especially if you are used to corporate environments and meeting rooms with whiteboards. If you are in the habit of using them to plan your work, use them to draw the map of your dream as well.
- **Post-its** – can be very effective too. Use a post-it to detail only one element of your map and make sure you have enough post-its to cover all of them. Each post-it should have only one item or a collection of related items on it. Then, as you finish drawing post-its one by one, you can stick them on a wall, a table or a big piece of paper – whatever works for you.
- **Mind mapping applications** – if you are the type who prefers to work on a computer, there are lots of great

tools for this purpose, including free ones. Simply search for "mind mapping applications" on Google and you'll find plenty of good results. Also, at the end of the book, we share some of our favourite applications, so that you can try them out yourself. The great thing about using mind mapping applications is that they are designed to facilitate the kind of map drawing we are encouraging you to do. Working with them is easy and requires no training at all if you are used to working with computers and office applications.

Slow Down and Look for . . .

The first iteration of your map is best done by yourself, in isolation from distractions like phones, e-mail, noise or other people. Use your home desk or any room where you can be alone to think and draw your own map. If it works for you, try to do it somewhere in the middle of nature or in a private cafe or tea house. You get the idea, right?

Being isolated from others will help you concentrate and draw a fairly complete map from the first try. Once you are done with it, take a break, relax for a while and then get back to your map, view it a couple of times and search for things like:

- **Questions left unanswered** – looking at each element in your map, are there any questions you feel are not answered? Try to identify if there are such questions and decide how you will answer them. Don't hesitate to update your map and include any elements required to answer your questions.

- **Missing connections between elements** – browse through your map and search for items that are not connected with others. You might have some steps that are not connected with their parent element or elements which are not connected to your dream. If that's the case, see if there is any reason for the missing connection (except for you forgetting to draw it). You might discover things you did not think through very well, which need more focus before you can connect them to the rest of the map in a logical way.

- **Elements that feel out of place** – is there anything on your map that doesn't feel right or simply feels like added extra you don't really need? We tend to embellish our dreams and add elements which are not really important. Also, you might draw elements or steps which overlap between themselves and only need to be done once. If you find such items, don't hesitate to remove them from your map and update it accordingly, so that the elements that make up the final version of the map are connected and make sense.

- **Elements that make you feel worried** – are there any conflicts between elements in your map? Are there too many things that need to be done at the same time? Do you need more money then you actually have? Do you need more time than you have at your disposal? For any conflicting item you identify, spend a bit more time thinking about your approach and redraw the map, if necessary. The idea here is to first identify what can be a source of problems, think about what you can do about it, make a decision and then update the map of your dream with how you will handle it.

- **Clearer ways of drawing ideas and elements** – you do not want to end up with a map drawn in a messy, chaotic way. You need to make sure every element included in the map is drawn in a clear and simple way, which helps you understand the map in its entirety. If you cannot make sense of something, you should redraw it, so that it is clear to you.

Keep Drawing

Now that you have your first version of the map, and you have identified the elements that need changing, it is time to redraw the map. However, you should not stop there. Take some time to relax, disconnect for a while and return a few hours or days later to your map. Expect it to take several iterations to get it to a state that is good enough for you to start working on your dream. When you update the map, don't think of the first version as wrong. See it as an essential stage in the evolution of your understanding of how to make your dream come true. The exercise of redrawing is not about the activity of drawing itself but the whole process of thinking, visualizing and improving your approach. This all improves while you keep drawing.

Remember though – it does not have to be perfect and you should not invest a lot of time in making too many maps. A map has to be clear enough so that you can make sense of your approach: you know where to begin, what to do for the next couple of weeks and you have identified the big challenges expected along the way. The map you are drawing must be a living entity. You should redraw it as you move forward and work on your dream. It should always show the path you will take for the next couple of weeks. The exercise of thinking and drawing should never stop, for as long as you work on making your dream come true the map should always be updated (or completely redrawn) based on what you learn along the way.

Also, we recommend that you keep your map drawings, at least the first and the newest version of it. If you keep the first map you've drawn and compare it with the last, drawn just before making your dream a reality, you will be amazed at the difference between them and how much you've learned and grown in the meantime.

How will I Know I've Done Well?

This is a very tough question to answer, as you never have a guarantee that your map is complete or that it includes all the important elements that need doing. Therefore, it is better to start working on your dream than to spend a huge amount of time on thinking and drawing.

However, from our experience, there are two factors that can help in the decision to stop drawing and start doing:

- **You are able to visualize the journey you are embarking on, in a way that makes sense.** If the map you have drawn makes sense and gives you reasonable clarity on what is required to make your dream come true, then you should move on. You don't need to dwell on clarifying each detail. You will learn as you go and you will adjust both your approach and the map.

- **You are able to stand up in front of someone you trust, but who knows nothing about your dream, and explain why you want to do it, what the dream is and how you will achieve it.** If you are able to go through this test, then you should definitely start working on making your dream come true. Stop refining or improving the map. Start working!

What Our Heroes Say

Alex

Alex has a larger dream to handle because of the complexity of what he is trying to achieve in becoming a Physician Scientist. Therefore his map is bigger than the others, with plenty of elements included. Not all of them are completely clarified but he has drawn each element at a level of detail he is comfortable to start with.

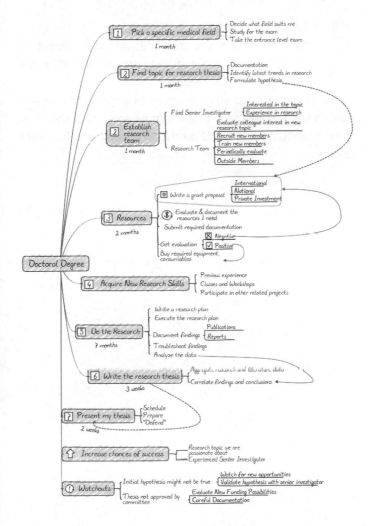

Doctoral Degree

1. **Pick a specific medical field** — 1 month
   - Decide what field suits me
   - Study for the exam
   - Take the entrance level exam

2. **Find topic for research thesis** — 1 month
   - Documentation
   - Identify latest trends in research
   - Formulate hypothesis

2. **Establish research team** — 1 month
   - Find Senior Investigator
     - Interested in the topic
     - Experience in research
   - Evaluate colleague interest in new research topic
   - Research Team
     - Recruit new members
     - Train new members
     - Periodically evaluate
     - Outside Members

3. **Resources** — 2 months
   - Write a grant proposal
     - International
     - National
     - Private Investment
   - Evaluate & document the resources I need
   - Submit required documentation
   - Get evaluation
     - Negative
     - Positive
   - Buy required equipment, consumables

4. **Acquire New Research Skills**
   - Previous experience
   - Classes and Workshops
   - Participate in other related projects

5. **Do the Research** — 7 months
   - Write a research plan
   - Execute the research plan
   - Document findings
     - Publications
     - Reports
   - Troubleshoot findings
   - Analyze the data

6. **Write the research thesis** — 3 weeks
   - Aggregate research and literature data
   - Correlate findings and conclusions

7. **Present my thesis** — 2 weeks
   - Schedule
   - Prepare
   - "Defend"

⬆ **Increase chances of success**
   - Research topic we are passionate about
   - Experienced Senior Investigator

⚠ **Watchouts**
   - Initial hypothesis might not be true
     - Watch for new opportunities
     - Validate hypothesis with senior investigator
   - Thesis not approved by committee
     - Evaluate New Funding Possibilities
     - Careful Documentation

Olive

Olive's map, as you can see, is quite different. It doesn't include too many elements but it is still more than enough to start well.

She did not want to add timings and deadlines to it as she doesn't want to approach this dream as something she must do in X amount of time and do this in parallel with her other priorities.

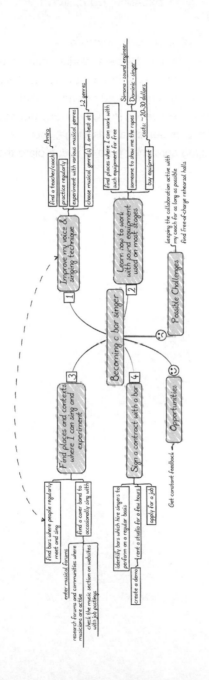

Becoming a bar singer

1 — Improve my voice & singing technique
- find a teacher/coach — *Amira*
- practice regularly
- experiment with various musical genres
- choose musical genre(s) I am best at — 1-2 genres

2 — Learn: how to work with sound equipment used on most stages
- find places where I can work with such equipment for free
- someone to show me the ropes — *Serena - sound engineer*, *Dominic - singer*
- buy equipment — costs: ~20-30 dollars

Possible Challenges 😕
- keeping the collaboration active with my coach for as long as possible
- find free-of-charge rehearsal halls

3 — Find places and contexts where I can sing and experiment
- find bars where people regularly meet and sing
  - enter musical forums
  - research forums and communities where musicians are active
- find a cover band to occasionally sing with
  - check the music section on websites with job postings

4 — Sign a contract with a bar
- identify bars which hire singers to perform on a regular basis
- create a demo
  - rent a studio for a few hours
  - apply for a job

Opportunities 🙂
- Get constant feedback

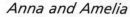

Anna and Amelia

Anna and Amelia worked hard to produce their map one sunny weekend. Just like Alex, their map is quite complex and includes plenty of elements. However, like Olivia, they did not impose any deadlines for themselves at this stage, they were more interested in making sure their map was complete than timed.

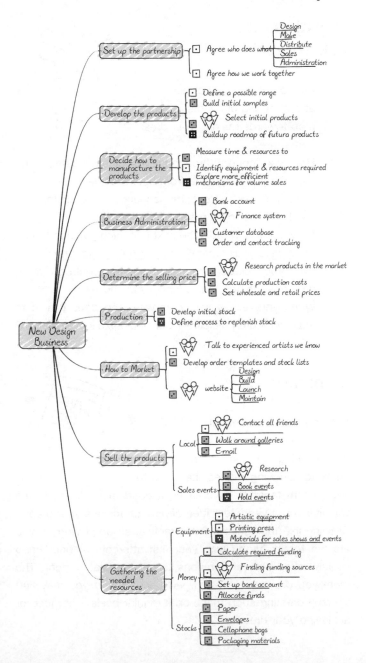

New Design Business

- Set up the partnership
  - Agree who does what
    - Design
    - Make
    - Distribute
    - Sales
    - Administration
  - Agree how we work together
- Develop the products
  - Define a possible range
  - Build initial samples
  - Select initial products
  - Buildup roadmap of future products
- Decide how to manufacture the products
  - Measure time & resources to
  - Identify equipment & resources required
  - Explore more efficient mechanisms for volume sales
- Business Administration
  - Bank account
  - Finance system
  - Customer database
  - Order and contact tracking
- Determine the selling price
  - Research products in the market
  - Calculate production costs
  - Set wholesale and retail prices
- Production
  - Develop initial stock
  - Define process to replenish stock
- How to Market
  - Talk to experienced artists we know
  - Develop order templates and stock lists
  - website
    - Design
    - Build
    - Launch
    - Maintain
- Sell the products
  - Local
    - Contact all friends
    - Walk around galleries
    - E-mail
  - Sales events
    - Research
    - Book events
    - Hold events
- Gathering the needed resources
  - Equipment
    - Artistic equipment
    - Printing press
    - Materials for sales shows and events
  - Money
    - Calculate required funding
    - Finding funding sources
    - Set up bank account
    - Allocate funds
  - Stocks
    - Paper
    - Envelopes
    - Cellophane bags
    - Packaging materials

Questions to Ask Yourself

- Are you reasonably clear about the big elements in your map towards making your dream come true?
- Have you thought through the resources you need, and the help you may need from other people?
- Have you worked out the sequence in which the elements of your dream should be done?
- Do you know what is the next first thing you need to do to achieve your dream? What about the second?
- Have you included the main things that could go wrong and those things that will help you succeed?
- When you review your complete map does it help to make your dream clearer? Can you make it even clearer?

Summary

Drawing is an essential part of turning your dream into reality, by consolidating and structuring your Thinking. Drawing makes the route to your dream tangible by creating a good map. A good map will give you a very clear idea of *how* to achieve your dream. Drawing like this takes a little practice, so don't worry if you are not totally happy with your first attempts. A good map usually takes several iterations to get completely right. The more you draw, the easier it will become and you may find yourself creating such maps on a regular basis – not just for achieving your dreams.

The secret of getting ahead is getting started.

Mark Twain

The Goal

When we look at people, we can categorize them into two general types. Firstly, there are those people who start things without thinking. Secondly, there are those who spend forever thinking and dreaming, but never actually start. What you should aim to achieve is a balance between those two extremes. If you have followed the first three chapters of this book, you should not make the first mistake. If you follow what we advise in this chapter, you should not make the second.

Starting sounds so easy but for many reasons it is often harder than you expect. People put off starting important things all the time. Common sense tells us all that you can't finish something unless you start it. But this is one of those pieces of common sense we are all guilty of ignoring regularly.

Don't Postpone!

Everybody, at times, puts off starting things we know we really ought to do NOW. We were all taught that the sooner we start something, the sooner it is over. But there are lots of things on a daily basis we put off and reschedule for a later date. Yet this should not be true for you and others reading this book.

You are about to fulfil a dream, and you have a map showing you how to achieve the dream. Surely you're going to get on with it now?

Hopefully yes, but in reality, the answer will often be no. Why is this? Why do we postpone even doing the things we really want to do? There are three reasons:

Reason 1 – You don't Want Your Dream Enough

Lots of people have dreams, or think they have dreams but just don't have the energy or enthusiasm to actually follow them through. There is a simple answer to this: you do not want your dream as much as you think you do. Laziness is something which applies to many areas of everyone's lives, but if you really want something, then you will find a way to overcome it.

Since you are reading this book, laziness is probably not such a big problem. The next two reasons though are the real issues that get in the way of even the least lazy person in the world: finding time and overcoming ourselves.

Reason 2 – You can't Find the Time

Finding the time to follow your dream can be a real problem. We strongly advise you not to keep putting off your dream until you think you will have the time to pursue it. People who do this tend to end up finding they never have the time to pursue their dreams.

Finding time can be hard. We suggest four ways to find some time:

- Firstly, analyze how you actually spend your time. All of us have wasted time in our lives – isn't your dream more important than watching TV or going to the cinema? We are not suggesting you live the life of a monk, but that if you really assess what you spend your time doing, you will find some time to pursue your dream.
- Secondly, prioritize how you spend your time. If you really want your dream to be real, it should be one of

your highest priorities. Achieving a dream can mean giving up some other less important activities, but you can always come back to them later. When you have to postpone some activity, do not choose those things associated with achieving your dream.

- Thirdly, a big problem can come from the important people around us. Following a dream can sometimes mean that people like partners, friends and family have less of our time. Most probably some of them won't like this. When you start out on your dream, try to strike a bargain with those people who are important in your life. Tell them your dream is really important to you, and for a period of time you need their support and understanding that this is where you will be focusing. Best of all, get them involved and excited by your dream too!

- Fourthly, use the time you have. If you have a free hour now – use it. When you find a spare day – work on your dream. Rarely will you find whole weeks or months free, but if you are lucky enough to have such time on your hands seize it. Never do nothing because you think "oh I need 3 months to do this, and I don't have 3 months free". If you think like this, chances are you will never have 3 months free and never achieve your dream. Successful people use up all those little gaps in their days and make progress towards their dreams, no matter how little.

Reason 3 – Ourselves

There is still one more problem which is much more of a challenge. The biggest impediment to getting dreams underway is *ourselves*.

Everyone has an internal dialogue going on in their heads all the time. This dialogue can be positive and helpful, but it also can be damaging and even destructive. One of the most common sensations when people start out on a dream is fear. Fear of what? Fear of the unknown. Fear of failure. Fear of making a fool of yourself.

The first thing to realize is that everyone has these feelings at times. Very few people are completely without doubt. But when you find yourself having these feelings, you have to force yourself to face up to them. When you face up to them, you will find that they often disappear.

Let's think about some of the things that stop people from moving forward:

- Fear of the unknown: this really should not bother you that much. This is your dream. Is it really that unknown? If it means doing new things – isn't that exciting? And as you move forward, you can go at your own pace and bring on the unknown as slowly or as quickly as you are willing to.
- Fear of failure: what can you actually fail at? No attempt to follow a dream is ever really a failure, even if you don't achieve your dream. All that happens is that you learn more and can work out other better ways to achieve this dream or even a better dream next time. There is no better teacher than personal experience, and you will never get to have personal experience if you don't try. In the end, wouldn't you rather be someone who has at least tried, failed and learned something than someone who didn't even try?
- Fear of making a fool of yourself: the only fools in life are those people who never try anything. The smartest and most successful people try lots of things, not always

successfully, but always learning from and usually enjoying the experience.

Of course, there may be real risks associated with your dream, such as losing a lot of money if you have to make a big investment. We don't want to trivialize this, but you must learn to differentiate between real risks and risks which exist only in your mind.

Making the First Step

If you want your dream enough, you will overcome laziness, find some time, and conquer your own fears.

What happens then? You start. You follow the first steps on your map. What will it be like? The next three chapters are going to help you keep going but, for now, we want to help you prepare for the feeling of those first steps.

The first thing is that it won't feel as you imagined. Don't be put off by this. This is simply because no matter how vivid your dream is and how clear your map, it is never exactly like reality. Feel the reality and enjoy it. Rather than being concerned, feel pleased with yourself that you are now moving ahead.

The fact that reality is never exactly the same as dreaming should be seen as a good thing, not a difficulty. As you move forward, you will find yourself learning and adapting.

The second thing is that pretty soon you will be faced with a problem that you have not foreseen. We will deal with this in the *Persevere* chapter. All we want to say now is: don't let problems put you off. Expect problems to show up and be willing to learn from them, adapt and improve your approach to making the dream come true. The reason that some people seem to achieve a lot isn't because they have no problems themselves, but because they are willing to do the work to solve them. Keep focused on your dream and keep moving towards it.

How will I Know I've Done Well?

It might seem that there is very little here to let you know that you've done well. After all, you have just taken your first step. What happens will be unique to you. But we find that when you start, the following tend to happen, (and they are all good signs as they mean progress is being made):

- **You feel a little emotional.** Maybe you will have that feeling that is a combination of enthusiasm intertwined with fear. Many people feel like this. As you move forward, the fear will slowly go away. On the other hand, perhaps you will feel a sense of relief – the *thinking* is over and now you are *doing*. If you don't feel any emotion, chances are you have not really started.
- **You will have done something.** Give yourself a pat on the back, even if it is just one small step and there are thousands to go. Celebrate! Even if you do it in a small way, like enjoying a glass of wine with your partner or best friend. Often, the first steps are the hardest. After a while, you will find yourself building momentum.
- **You will have learnt something.** It may be something very small, but at every step you learn more both

about the dream and yourself. Don't lose this learning – it is valuable. Every time you make progress think about it and reflect on what you have learnt.

- **Something will have gone wrong.** This may sound like an odd thing to say now, but it is usually true that something goes wrong pretty soon after starting. Don't worry, everyone experiences this. It is not until something goes wrong, and you find a way to solve the problem, that you are really moving. Best of all don't think of these as problems – but merely as variances between your map and reality. A variance that you will find a way of working around.

What Our
Heroes Say

Alex
We manage to catch up with Alex on a sunny afternoon and we are lucky to be able to sit outside in the sunshine and talk to him.

1. How did you start?

First, I had to pick the medical field in which I wanted to become specialized. This was something I was working on anyway, when we started our discussions. There weren't any important first steps for me to take on this, except making the decision about the field to choose, which ended up being the field of pulmonology, or respiratory as it is called in some countries.

For me, the real start of this dream was when I managed to find an initial research team and we started work on identifying the topic for our research thesis.

There were six of us (both students and teachers) – all knowing we needed to work together on a great research project that would allow us – the students – to get the specialization we dreamed of. We had no idea of exactly what research topic we would cover, but we knew we had to find something worthwhile.

We searched the speciality literature for interesting topics and trends to cover, chose some theories that seemed worth pursuing and made some initial experiments to see where they got us. The trouble is that all our experiments failed and got us nowhere. Nothing was confirming the hypothesis we drafted initially.

2. That's a tough way to start. What did you do next?

We all panicked and had no idea what to do next. That's why we called in the senior investigator, who had agreed to sponsor our research, for help. With his help, we successfully changed our methodology for making a research hypothesis and the way we made rough experiments, to confirm we were looking in the right direction. After a few days we were doing a lot less trial and error based experiments. We now had a "method to our madness", a method that was getting us closer to where we wanted to be: finding an exciting research hypothesis that was worth investigating and was interesting enough for us to obtain the funding and resources required to work on it.

3. Did you succeed in finding it?

Yes we did. But it wouldn't have been possible without the help we received from our senior investigator.

Olive

We meet Olive late one evening. It has been a long day for all of us and at first the conversation is slow. But once Olive gets talking we all get excited about finding out the journey to her dream has really started.

1. How did you start?

   It happened by chance, before we started our conversations about this dream and a better way of working on it. As I said before, this is an old dream of mine and I had recently I met a canto teacher – Amira – with whom I became friends. She listened to me singing a couple of times and said that I have what it takes to become a real singer. I started working on this dream when she said she wanted to coach me, help me improve and learn more about being a real singer. Only then did I start to do some real thinking about what this dream will take to become reality: the steps involved, the things I need, etc.

2. So, Amira was the catalyst that made you take this dream more seriously than before?

   Yes, she was. With her help, I was able to clarify the best way to start and the important steps I need to take. Talking with her, seeing her confidence in me and the fact that I can accomplish this dream, meant a lot and gave me the confidence to actually start.

3. So, how were the first steps you made?

   They were hard. I started by singing in karaoke bars. At that time I had quite a few fears: the fear of singing in public surrounded by strangers, the fear of singing in an unfamil-

iar place, the fear of my singing not being enjoyed by others.

4. How did you get past your fears?

    While going to these bars, I studied a bit the people that generally go there to sing. I noticed that many of them had a passion for singing, wanted similar things to what I want, from a musical perspective, and shared the same shyness and fears. So, I felt safer and sang more and more. I noticed that people were actually trying to be supportive, that it is OK to make mistakes and I can actually learn from them.

Anna and Amelia

We meet Anna and Amelia in Anna's home town of Cheltenham, where we ask them about how they came to start their business.

1. Tell us about how you came to start the business?

   Well, it took longer than we expected! It must have been about 2 years before we actually started the business that Amelia made some cards for Christmas. They were beautiful and people who received them (including Anna), started to keep them and even frame them as pictures. We were having a social conversation and we realized that we both wanted to start a small business. In the conversation we thought Amelia's cards would be a good product to start a business with. As we talked further, we came to realize that we would like to work together to run this business.

2. Why did it take 2 years from discussion to starting?

   It was just the everyday things in life that got in the way. Plus at some point, both of us had elderly relatives to support. This went on for a while. We were getting frustrated. So we talked, and we realized we just had to make it real. We had to start, even if it was very slow to begin with. Else we might delay it forever!

3. So what was it like starting?

   It was great, a little nerve racking, but at the same time a relief, as we had been talking about it for so long. We started slowly: talking, thinking and working out what needed to be done to really set up the business.

4. Did you want to go faster?

To some extent yes, but funnily enough there was a big advantage in going slowly. We needed time to allow ourselves the opportunity to explore ideas and come up with creative concepts. We had time to do some informal market research: what was selling online, in shops and in galleries? Was there anything like our cards? What sort of price were equivalent products selling for and so on? If we had forced ourselves to a deadline too early, we might not have got this far. There is something very liberating about not forcing yourself along a fixed timeline, as long as you are making progress.

But once we had our ideas sorted – both for the products and how we would sell them – we started moving faster. Now we work to deadlines, many of which are set by external events such as having a collection ready for a trade show.

5. How did the business launch?

We more or less simultaneously launched our website and emailed everyone we knew about the business. We planned to launch the business in September, to be ready to sell cards for Christmas. In the end, we were a month late because the website took longer to develop than we expected.

6. Is there anything else you would add about starting?

Yes, we think one thing is very important for a partnership. To make it work, you have to understand each other's pace of work, strengths and weaknesses. If one of you is always pressing for timelines while the other is not bothered how long it will take, it will not work. It's a partnership and you have to flex to each other's style.

The other thing is that we both admit it would have been better to have started earlier. We both had valid reasons for not starting, but you have to start sooner or later. On the other hand, once we started, it was right to go slowly.

Because we allowed ourselves to go slowly at first, it was easier for us to find the time to make progress. So we would advise anyone else to be realistic about the amount of time they have and then make as much or as little progress as they can in that time. You can wish forever that you have more time, it's far better to use what you have, even if it is not much.

Questions to Ask Yourself

- Am I certain that I want this specific dream enough?
- Where can I find the time to pursue the dream?
- Am I really challenging myself to make the time available? Am I really seizing all those moments when I could work on my dream?
- Is my internal dialogue holding me back from my own dreams?
- Are my doubts and fears less compelling than the thought of achieving my dream?
- Have I actually started? If not, why not?

Summary

Often the reason people don't achieve their dreams is that they never start! You may not have started on your dreams because deep down you don't want the dream you are thinking about enough. Explore your feelings more closely, as you will only find the energy and drive to achieve the dreams you really want. Alternatively, you may not have started because you cannot find the time. By analyzing how you spend your time and grabbing hold of all the gaps you have you will find more time than you expect. Finally, you may not have started on your dream because of yourself and your own internal dialogue stopping you making progress. You have it within yourself to overcome personal doubts. Fears of the unknown, failure, or making a fool of yourself can be overcome.

The rather obvious, but critically important guideline is simply – *if you don't ever start you will never finish*. By starting you are moving from just Dreaming to Doing, and are on the way to making your dream reality.

5   PROGRESS

All great masters are chiefly distinguished by the power of adding a second, a third, and perhaps a fourth step in a continuous line.

Ralph Waldo Emerson

The Goal

This chapter helps you in the most important, but sometimes most underestimated, part of achieving your dreams: making progress.

Making progress can seem to be the easiest part of achieving your dream compared to what we discuss in other chapters. You have a well thought through dream, you have a map, you have started – so isn't it now just a case of keeping going? And isn't keeping going pretty easy? Well, yes and no.

There is a challenge in making progress and continuing to make progress. We all know people who are fantastic at doing the things they set out to do. But many people start on their dreams full of enthusiasm and energy, but somehow the dream is never achieved. We want to help you become one of those people who always manage to finish what they set out to do.

The Way to Make Progress

There is a very simple set of things you need to do to make progress. Of course, real life makes things complex, but if you keep this simple set of things in mind you will not go too far wrong. The things you need to do are:

1. Refer to your map: where are you going next?
2. Work: make a step towards your dream, based on your map.
3. Reflect. Did that step work? Did it move you forward or not? What can you learn from it?

4. Take more steps. You should be aiming to get into a rhythm. We all have our own rhythms that suit us personally and our circumstances. This rhythm is never perfectly even and steady, but making good progress towards a dream is much more like running a marathon than a sprint. Marathon runners each have their own rhythm. Ideally, take a step, even if it is a very small one, every day.
5. Check back to your map. Are you getting where you need to? If you are, that's perfect. If not, think why not and then either modify your approach or improve your map.
6. Keep going through activities 1–5 again and again, until you reach your dream.

Does this seem too simple? Well, in a way it is, and in the rest of this chapter and the book we build on this model and refine it. Nevertheless, the real truth about making progress towards your dream is that the underlying way you do this is very simple – you take a series of steps, one step at a time. It is the accumulation of steps that gets you to your end point.

Characteristics of Progress Makers

If making progress is that simple, what is it that enables some people to keep progressing, whilst others never get to their dreams? Here's a list of a few personal characteristics to help you think about yourself and learn how to be great at making progress.

People who achieve their dreams are:

*   **Activity oriented:** progress never occurs unless you do something. Progress makers are driven to action all

the time. When there is an opportunity to do something, they do it. Contrast this with other people who suffer from what we call *inertia*. These people can never get the momentum of progress going, and are always finding reasons not to take the next step. When progress makers have a spare hour, they don't watch TV or read what others have said on Facebook – they are either taking a step or reviewing their map. If you want to achieve your dreams, take a step, then another and then another! It is the only way.

- **Outcome focused:** being activity oriented is great, but it needs to be supported by an outcome focus. Activity needs to lead somewhere. To take a good step, you don't need to look at your feet very often; you need to look towards where you are going. You have a map showing the way. Use it.

- **Driven and flexible:** great progress makers are driven. They don't lose interest after a few hard days or when the first problems arise. They continue to push forward. But pushing forward is not about blindly going down one route if it is not working. Great progress makers are flexible. They adapt when their plans do not work, and do more of the things they find that do work.

These three factors are the most important. But achieving your dreams, especially if those dreams are big or complex, can require more than this. We want to add two other factors which will also help you make progress:

- **Having fun:** it's true that not everyone enjoys the process of getting to their dreams, and it is inevitable that even the most fun loving person will find some days better than others. But we firmly believe that having fun whilst you make progress is really important. It will help to keep you motivated, and it just makes life better! If there are two ways to get something done, choose the one that is more fun. Even if this sometimes means it takes a bit longer.

- **Learning as you go along:** this is one of the most important points in this chapter. All of us make mistakes. None of us knows the right way to do everything. If we do get there the first time, often it has more to do with luck than wisdom. Many successful people have failed several times before achieving their dreams. What really differentiates the achievers in life from the underachievers is that the achievers learn. And as they learn, they adapt their approach. You should feel no shame in changing your map as you progress. It is foolish to keep doing the same thing all the time when your experience gives you the opportunity to learn and improve.

Lessons Learned the Hard Way

So far in this chapter we have picked out some of the more straightforward points about making progress. We really believe in the simple picture we have painted, but it would be wrong to suggest that there are not some more sophisticated points about making progress.

We want to give you some lessons that come from our and our friends' experiences of working towards dreams. These lessons have mostly been learnt the hard way – we only learnt them after we got things wrong! But we want you to learn from our experiences and hopefully have a smoother journey.

1. **Don't mistake being busy with making progress.** Of course, achieving your dream may require you often to be very busy, but being busy as a result of following your map. It is not a valuable outcome in itself. Many people feel pleased with themselves when they have had a busy day and have done lots of things. But unless those things are moving you towards your dream, they are pointless. I'm sure you will have seen people who are always busy, but never seem to get anything done. All of us fall into this trap at times, and it is a trap to avoid. You want to be busy – but purposefully busy.

2. **The straightest line is not always the best.** This might seem counterintuitive, but our experience shows it to be true. Straight lines are the shortest way between two points – but you can't always go in a straight line, and sometimes you should not even try. The most direct route may require you to face all sorts of difficulties and challenges that can be avoided if you go in a different direction. The most direct route may not make the best use of your personal skills and the resources you have. On the other hand, you do need to be making progress towards your dream. You can't just wander all over the place. So, we have the concept of *purposeful wandering*. That is sometimes taking detours, not always forcing yourself to go in a straight line – but doing so in a deliberate way, and always with an eye to your map and achieving your dream.

3. **Remember to stop and measure your success.** If you have a good day's work, and you take 10 steps towards achieving your dream, then you deserve to feel pleased with yourself and give yourself a pat on the back. But never forget: it is not how far you have gone that is important in achieving dreams, but *how far you*

have to go. Unless you are getting relentlessly closer to your dream, you are being a busy fool.

How will I Know If I've Done Well?

There are lots of ways to measure progress. If you talk to business people, or professional project manag-ers, they can describe all sorts of complex ways to know that you are making progress. In most personal situations, you don't need them!

There are four simple things that will tell if you are doing well:

- **You are getting closer to your dream.** Maybe not every day, and not in every action. But over time you are relentlessly moving forward.
- **Your progress has a rhythm.** You don't work on your dream 1 day every 6 months, but you take regular, fre-quent steps. For example, you work on your dream each weekend or 1 full day each week. You have created a regular schedule for working on your dream that doesn't conflict with your other priorities and dreams and gives you a rhythm for making constant progress.
- **You are learning and improving your map** as you move ahead. The map you have drawn initially is con-stantly being refined and improved.
- **You are enjoying yourself.** Maybe not every day and with every step, but overall you take pleasure in making progress and feeling your dream getting closer.

What Our Heroes Say

Alex

It's harder than usual to track Alex down for our next interview, but we think this is probably a good sign – a sign that Alex is working hard and progressing.

1. What progress have you made so far?

   We are close to finishing the work on the third big element on our map – getting all the resources we need for conducting our research. We finished writing the grant proposal and applied for funding to a national grant funding committee. We should receive an answer to our application in the next week or so.

2. That sounds encouraging. Did you manage to create a rhythm for making progress on this dream?

   Yes we did. We agreed to work in parallel, each with their own experiments, different to the other members of the team.

   We regularly meet once per week to discuss our findings, results and problems and we decide together how we go about taking the next steps. Having a weekly meeting also serves as a deadline, motivating us to have our current piece of work ready by the next time we meet. If most team members have done their part and I haven't, it would make me feel bad and I would have let them down. We found this to be a great motivator to keep going and make a bit of progress each week.

3. How do you make sure you are making real progress?

    If we were not making real progress, we would not have so much preliminary data to show that our research thesis is going in the right direction. We would not have real data, documented results or problems to overcome. If we did not make real progress, it would be very obvious, very quickly. At least some of our team members would notice it and raise this in our meetings.

4. How is the spirit within the team? Are you enjoying the work you do together, do you get along well?

    I'm happy to see that our team is excited and involved in this common dream of ours. We feel that we are working on something worthwhile and, at least so far, we've made a good amount of progress at a very good pace.

    One thing that helps is that we do our best to be as light hearted as possible, especially when we encounter issues in our work. We always expect at least some minor problems to show up. We try to discuss these openly and help each other. What we've learned so far is that we are a diverse team, each with a different combination of experience, medical and research knowledge. Therefore we find it helpful to have open discussions and easier to find solutions together than on our own.

Olive

We catch up with Olive in the morning of a grey day. The greyness seems dispiriting, but Olive is lively and full of energy. Over a coffee we discuss how she is progressing.

1. What progress have you made so far?

    If you look at my map, I am working on the second element: learning how to work with the sound equipment used on a typical stage. I made quite a few experiments with various musical genres and chose the two I consider myself best at singing. Also, I have done quite a few rehearsals and met with my coach a couple of times.

2. Did you manage to create a rhythm for making progress on this dream?

    I created a rhythm through my canto lessons and rehearsals in karaoke bars. I am doing this more often than I used to when I first started. Beating my fears about making a fool of myself helped me a lot in being able to sing more in public.

    The simple act of going to karaoke bars each week makes me do rehearsals at home, on my own, so that the next time I sing in public, I perform better.

3. Are you sure you are making real progress and not just fooling yourself?

    Yes, I am. It shows through the feedback I receive from people. Now it is more about nuances and special things I can improve, which most people (or at least those who are not very passionate about music) won't notice as being shortcomings in my singing.

Also, when I sing in karaoke bars, I see people responding to my singing and appreciating my performance. Because of this, I feel more confident in my singing abilities and I think I have a real chance of making this dream come true.

4. What have you learned so far?

I realized that one of the best tools for improving my singing was to record myself and then listen to the way I sing. I am able to notice more easily what I do well and what I don't do so well. I thought this might help at the beginning, but I had no idea how much of an impact it would have on my learning. I plan to do this regularly in the future.

Anna and Amelia

We met up with Anna and Amelia, in Anna's house in the English countryside. It is one of those overcast dull days that are common in the winter in England. But it seems warm and busy in the house.

1. Are you making progress?

   Anna: *Yes we are, but not as fast as I would like.*
   Amelia: *Yes, I'd say the same. I have some new designs for cards and I have started to make some more prints as there was demand for these at our first trade show, but I have a lot to do to be ready for the next one.*

2. How do you know you are making real progress?

   Anna: *It's a tricky question. I have a day-to-day list of things to do, and I have our overall map of where we should be going. But right now, while I am progressing, it has slowed down. Sometimes it almost feels as if it has stalled. This is both for personal reasons (my father is rather ill) and also because of other work going on. However, if I look backwards I can see how far we have come – it's just not as quick as I would like.*
   Amelia: *Like Anna I have interruptions, but it's more straightforward for me. I have a lot to do, but it's very clear what I need to move forward with. For Anna it's harder, as she has a wider range of tasks – really everything on the business and sales side.*

3. How will you get back to the speed you want?

   Anna: *That will be difficult over the next few weeks, but we have a fixed date we must meet in terms of our next* *trade show in 3 weeks' time. This puts pressure on us, but it forces us to work irrespective of other interruptions. So in that way it is helpful. And I need to remember that I have completed lots of things in my diary. These things may not directly progress our dream, but I have removed lots of barriers to progress. So, I am getting into a position where I can dedicate 4 days a week to the dream, for a while. It really needs this level of focus to get our sales going. I have a large number of leads to follow up that I have not been able to work on for the last few weeks.*

4. Do you have a good rhythm?

    Amelia: *We had a good rhythm, but we have lost it a little, and we both accept that this is a problem. The good thing about working as partners is that we can talk to each other and motivate each other. I think we are getting back to our rhythm, but it has definitely been a slow month. I think having our map and really being aware of the dream, and what we need to do to achieve it, helps a lot, as it gives us something to guide ourselves towards doing things rather than just dreaming. Even when it is slow, we are progressing.*

5. Is there anything you have learnt so far?

    Anna: *The main thing is that when you work with suppliers and when you are dependent on other people – always leave plenty of time. I have found many suppliers to be really slow and needing constant chasing. If I need something simple off the Internet, then that can be quick. But, for example, recently I bought some lights for exhibitions. They took ages to come, then they didn't work, so I had to return to the supplier to get new ones. This sort of thing is not unusual! Even things you think should be very easy* *and quick often take time. Your own work is quick – but always make sure there is more time available than you think is necessary.*

Amelia: *The other thing is sometimes progress is indirect. So you may not be working on the dream itself, but finishing off or clearing out other tasks which are getting in the way of progress.*

6. How are you feeling?

Anna: *In reality we are both very optimistic and positive. We have recently made some small sales, and we are working closely with one prestigious client. So it's going in the right direction and it feels good!*

Questions to Ask Yourself

- What am I going to do *today* to work on my dream?
- Am I doing things that help me achieve progress?
- Am I taking steps on a frequent and regular basis?
- Am I following and improving my map?
- Is my route the best route for me, even if it is not the straightest?
- Am I learning, and is what I am learning showing me better ways?
- Am I enjoying this adventure?

Summary

The central part of getting anything done is to make progress in the right direction, as guided by your map. Your aim should be to be making progress continuously, ideally some progress every day and to a regular rhythm. People who are good at making effective progress tend to be activity orientated and outcome focused as well as being driven and flexible. Additionally, it will help you make progress if you have fun and learn as you go along. But don't mistake progress for just being busy. You need to be busy to make progress, but busy in the right way when you can see yourself moving forward on your map.

6 PERSEVERE

Great works are performed not by strength but by perseverance.

Samuel Johnson

The Goal

Problems are a part of everyday life. You should expect to encounter them when working on any worthwhile dream. The more challenging the dream, the more frequent and difficult the problems you encounter will be. The larger your ambitions, the more dependent you will be on your ability to overcome problems and learn from mistakes.

The good news is that very few problems are truly insurmountable. Also, many problems are artificial, in the sense that we create them by allowing panic to grip us and take control. When we encounter a problem, we fail to spend time thinking about what really happened, why it happened, how we could overcome the problem and, most of all, learn from it.

Persevering at accomplishing your dreams takes courage and effort. In this chapter we would like to help, by making you realize that problems are normal and they can be solved. We want to encourage you to expect them as something ordinary and show ways to learn from them. Following the advice we share will significantly increase your chances of success with each problem you overcome and learn from.

The Sources of Most Problems

Problems are obstacles, difficulties and situations that need resolution in order for us to achieve the outcome we desire. They are generally caused by our mistakes and failures at achieving some of the things we need or want.

Even though problems can be caused by lots of different factors, there are certain factors that tend to be at the root of most problems we encounter. Here are a few questions worth asking yourself regularly, to make sure you have the best chance of identifying problems sooner rather than later:

- **Am I really doing the work?** It does not make any sense to lie to yourself or be too lax in evaluating your own work. Are you making real, measurable progress in doing the work you've drawn up for yourself? Most times, when we don't achieve the desired outcomes and we have problems, it is simply because we are not engaged enough in doing the real work required to accomplish our dreams. Being lazy and indulgent with yourself for more than a few days does not help in avoiding problems and achieving your dream.

- **Am I aware of the resources I need to get the next steps done?** When we start working on our dreams, we have a limited understanding of the resources we need to get everything done. As you work and learn along the way, ask yourself regularly about the resources you need for the next steps you are about to take. There's always some little thing that might have been missed at the beginning. Make sure you have it available when it's needed and not later.

- **Do the people who help me have the same level of understanding about what needs to be done and what has recently changed?** Communication between people tends to be the weakest link in everything we do. We assume that people have understood us, even though we do not provide much detail about what we need them to do. We assume they are aware of something we regard as common knowledge. We assume that they know about a recent change that impacts what needs to be done. Making the effort to double check things, especially if you feel that communication has not been clear enough, helps avoid problematic situations. Making fewer assumptions contributes to good communication about what is important and relevant.

- **Am I being paranoid?** Some people overthink the things that might happen. This can be the case when we try so hard to avoid failure or making mistakes that we get stuck worrying. Being obsessive about some aspects of what might happen can stir up problems which would not exist otherwise. The fear of failure often stops us giving our best to our dreams. Try to stop yourself each time you notice yourself over-thinking and over-worrying – and get back to making progress!

Avoiding Problems

There is a simple and effective tactic that can help you avoid most problems. Make sure that from time to time you think about two important questions we asked in the earlier stages of this book:

- What is most likely to go wrong and what can I do to avoid this?
- What would increase my chances of success?

Every time you make meaningful progress and clarify additional details on your map, consider these questions. When you do this, think about the context you are in, what has changed since you started and what is most likely to change in the future. With progress you are better able to answer these questions. You know more about what it takes to achieve your dream, what works, what does not work and what is more likely to fail.

Also, the experience you have gathered so far makes you better at spotting opportunities that will increase your chances of success. Taking advantage of these opportunities goes a long way towards avoiding problems. You can gain more confidence as you learn valuable lessons that contribute to your success.

Solving Problems

The key to fixing a problem is making sure you first understand it, instead of letting fear and confusion take the lead. There is nothing worse than flailing around, in a state of panic, trying to fix something you don't fully understand. This will always make things worse and won't lead to a constructive outcome.

Here are a few recommendations that will help solve most problems you encounter:

- **If you have strong feelings about what has just happened, take some time to unwind and cool down.** You can try things like: visiting a place that makes you feel relaxed, doing something you enjoy, taking a short walk etc.
- **Explain what just happened to someone you trust.** The exercise of talking not only makes you calmer, but gives you the chance to identify mistakes you might miss if you only have an internal dialogue about the problem that happened. Think about the chronology of events as best as you can remember. Go through all the details, including those that seem minor and, most of all, listen to other people's observations.
- **If you are working with several people at achieving something, make sure you talk with each**

person about what happened. Listen to their views of what happened, compare it with your own and pay attention to the points of difference between views. These conversations can help reveal important gaps that contributed to your problem.

- **Validate the assumptions you made when you started working on the things that have failed.** We have the tendency to assume something is true and while spending little or no time validating its truthfulness. Many problems are caused by assuming the wrong things when we start to work.

- **Once you understand what happened, do not blame yourself or others.** Focusing on whose fault it was does not lead to a constructive outcome. Do your best to focus on the most positive outcome you can obtain, given the situation. Think about what's the best way to move forward and solve the problem as soon as possible.

- **Take the time to talk and internalize the lessons you've learned.** What will you do in the future to avoid similar situations? Don't assume the lesson was learned without at least having a discussion about it. The more uncomfortable you feel talking about the problem, the more important it is that you do this.

Quit the Wrong Tactics

One of the things successful people do is quickly deciding what and when to quit. Despite what we've been taught in school and by parents, quitting is good, as long as we don't quit our dreams. Quit the wrong tactics, not the dream itself. Every day we make mistakes that allow us to learn what works and what does not. Mistakes, more than successes, are what keep the human race moving forward, evolving and growing at an amazing pace.

When working on your dream, expect that everyone involved will make mistakes. Mistakes can have a positive outcome if you learn quickly, adjust and become more successful at achieving your dream. Making a mistake does not make you a failure. Failing to learn from mistakes and adjusting your approach makes you a failure.

It is important to keep an eye on the problems you regularly encounter. They are a sign of repeated mistakes or the wrong tactics being applied, which were not spotted quickly enough and from which you have not learnt.

If you start encountering a problem that seems to be re-occurring, or you notice a pattern to your problems, it means you have not noticed important mistakes you keep making. If this happens to you, apply the recommendations we shared for solving problems and think about the overall approach you have taken so far. Talk about it with other people and, as soon as you identify what you are doing wrong, quit doing it. As Albert Einstein reportedly said: *"Insanity is doing the same things over and over again and expecting different results."*

Don't be afraid to adjust your approach and see what happens. Most times you won't need to make big changes. Minor improvements can lead to great results and higher chances of success.

Do Not Quit Your Dream

Do not quit your dream because you have encountered a problem and have no idea what to do next. Be patient with

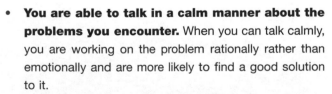

yourself and others, take the time to figure it out. If necessary, quit the wrong tactics you applied so far, but do not quit your dream. As Jonas Salk said: *"There is no such thing as failure. Only giving up too soon."*

As you work and learn, you will improve your understanding of your dream, the outcome you expect and what you should do to get there. We recommend that you make improvements each time you learn something valuable. Improving a dream is great, quitting one is not. It only makes your fears grow, lowers your confidence and your opportunity for growth as a human being. The more you get into the habit of quitting your dreams, the less likely you will be able to accomplish any of your dreams.

How will I Know I've Done Well?

Here are a few signs that you are doing well at persevering and handling the mistakes and the problems you encounter:

- **You are able to talk in a calm manner about the problems you encounter.** When you can talk calmly, you are working on the problem rationally rather than emotionally and are more likely to find a good solution to it.
- **You still have a sense of humour.** If you are able to have a laugh at your own mistakes, it means you have accepted your mistakes, learned from them and moved on.

- **You have a good understanding of what you will change in the future**, so that you avoid the problems you've encountered so far.
- **You are excited about what's next**, to take the next steps in achieving your dream and seeing what happens.
- **You will become increasingly confident** that as problems arise you will be able to solve them.
- **You will not have an ever growing set of problems.** New problems may arise, but old problems will remain resolved.

What Our
Heroes Say

Alex

As usual when we meet Alex, he is busy. We interrupt his work for as short a period as possible, just to get some updates and understand the problems he has faced and how he has resolved them.

1. What are the problems you encountered so far?

   There are two important problems we have encountered so far:

   - *Very soon after we started, we realized we needed to have a bigger team than the six of us that started initially. We recruited four new students to join us and we started the work. Unfortunately, some of them quickly lost interest. They stopped joining our meetings, sometimes without even notifying the rest of the team. Therefore, for a while, we did not make as much progress as we wanted.*

   - *At one point we had issues with funding the preliminary research work required to create the grant proposal. For a few weeks we did not have enough materials and substances to get our initial research experiments done. This meant we were not able to make valuable progress during that time and finish our grant proposal.*

2. Those are big problems, especially so early in your work on the dream. How did you go about solving them?

   Regarding our staffing problem, we realized that the solution was to recruit new people one at a time. We talked with other students and some agreed to join us. This meant we needed to spend additional time training them, giving them all the background on what we are trying to do and what we have done so far.

Also, to make sure we avoided similar problems with our new team mates, the more "senior" members of our team spent more time coaching them in the beginning. More than we did in the past with the previous members. This helped a lot and since then we have not encountered similar problems with our team.

The funding was a tricky problem to solve. For a while we were afraid that we would not find a solution. Again, we went to our senior investigator and asked for help. Luckily for us, he came through once more. With his help, we managed to get in touch with people interested in our research thesis and received a bit of private investment to fund our work. It was enough for us to finish all the preparation for writing the grant proposal.

3. Now that you have solved these problems, is everything OK? Is there anything else impeding your progress?

   No, there's not. Now and then some experiments fail but that's nothing out of the ordinary. Such failures are a normal component of research work and we solve them as a team.

4. Do you feel confident about what's next?

   Yes, I do. We all do. The new team works well together. As I said in our previous discussion, we are all excited by where we are going with our research.

   Recently, we've had good results from our research. Also, even though we have not yet received the final answer regarding our application for funding, there are people who have noticed our work. They are excited by what we've done so far and, most probably, we will receive a positive answer very soon.

Olive

We meet up with Olive back at her apartment in a late afternoon. She is happy to see us and share her views, but she seems a bit less up-beat than usual. Let's find out what is worrying her.

1. What are the problems you encountered so far?

   There are two important problems that have shown up so far:

   - *The first and most important is that I have had to quit my job, without having an offer for a position in another company. So many chaotic changes were made by my former employer that I couldn't take it anymore and had to quit. It was no longer an environment in which I enjoyed working. Now, my top priority is to find a better position in a company that is less chaotic and self-destructive.*
   - *Another problem is that, lately, my canto teacher and I have had problems finding the time required to meet and go through the usual lessons. This has been caused by conflicting schedules and priority changes for the both of us.*

2. How do they impact your progress?

   Unfortunately, in the last 2 or 3 weeks, I've made less progress than before. Right now, my first priority is to find a good job. I'm spending most of my time and energy brushing up my resume, applying for positions at different companies that interest me, going to interviews, etc. As soon as I solve this problem, I will be less stressed and be able to invest more time and energy into this dream. Feeling unsure about my financial and professional future has made me less motivated to work on it.

3. Did you quit working on your dream due to these problems?

   I did not. I am simply doing less work on making it come true. I have not gone to canto lessons for the last few days but I have continued practising by myself, recording what I sing and listening carefully to my performance. I've also kept singing in karaoke bars, but slightly less often than before, because of the uncertain financial situation I am in at the moment. At least, until I find another job.

4. What about finding the time to go to canto lessons again?

   I am keeping in touch with my teacher. She has been through a chaotic period recently and hasn't had the time to see me. The next time I talk to her, I will try to schedule the next lesson.

5. Have you considered asking her to schedule some regular lessons, but this time paid instead of free? This might convince her to give more priority to your lessons, considering that she would have a financial gain from your collaboration?

   It is an idea worth trying but I need to find a job first. Depending on how fast I solve this problem and how our relationship continues, I might consider doing this.

6. Good luck in solving these problems. The next time we talk, we hope you will have more good news to share.

   Thank you!

Anna and Amelia

Anna and Amelia have been working on their dream for some months now. It's time to catch up and find out how they are getting along and what unexpected problems they have had to face. As we enter Amelia's house for our interview, we can smell freshly baked cake. We are looking forward to this meeting!

1. You have been working on your dream for some time now, what sort of problems have you encountered?

   There have been lots of things we didn't expect, that we have had to sort out as we've gone along, but we think there have been four most significant problems:

   1. *Lack of sufficient time to attend to all aspects of our dream to the level we want to.*
   2. *Financial constraints – limits to the amount of money we can spend to achieve our dream.*
   3. *Dealing with incompetent or unprofessional suppliers and poor service generally.*
   4. *Finding the right way to identify and approach customers and getting known in the right circles.*

2. That seems quite a range of issues, how have you gone about solving them?

   We have sorted out each of these problems in different ways. Some of them we have resolved, others we have fixed for a while but need to come back to again to find better solutions:

   1. *Problem 1 is not fully resolved. We both try to prioritize our time on working on our dream. We look at our map regularly and we talk to motivate each other. We are*

getting better at managing our time, but we are far from perfect!

2. *Problem 2 is solved for now. We found a member of the family who is willing to back us for a while. We will need to pay him back, but he has been very flexible and we can take as much time as we need to return the money. There are not limitless funds, but we don't need too much. He has given us enough to get going.*

3. *Problem 3 is ongoing. It is amazing how poor many suppliers are. We have learnt never to leave anything requiring an outside supplier to the last minute, as you cannot rely on them. So we plan ahead more and engage suppliers as soon as we start to think about using them. Then, if they don't deliver or deliver late, we have time to deal with it. We are getting better at choosing suppliers and we have stopped working with those who gave us a poor service.*

4. *Problem 4 is ongoing but we have learnt lots. We have experimented with different ways of approaching customers. Some work and some don't, but we have learnt some great things. We ask everyone we know, family and friends and anyone we meet in business: How do you approach customers? How do you like to be sold to? All sorts of questions like that. We are always asking. It is great how often people are willing to help and give advice on this topic.*

3. That's really interesting, and helps us understand how you have solved specific problems, but how you do deal with problems in general?

We are lucky in that there are two of us, so we always can discuss problems and try to work out ways around them. Two brains really are much better than one. We also involve

*family and friends for advice and ideas on how to over-
come big challenges – and we have been given some great
ideas.*

*Occasionally, we have been guilty of ignoring problems.
Which is not very good! But on the other hand, some
problems really should be left for the time being. Every day
we have to prioritize and sometimes we have a problem
but it won't impact us today. We are aware of it, but we
do nothing because it is not a priority today. However,
when we come back to it later, we often find a solution.
It's like our brains are working on it in the background
whilst we get on with other things.*

*If you focus too much on fixing problems all the time,
you can forget about getting on with the things you can
progress, and this really dissipates your energy. Focus on
the solutions and making progress where you can and
most of the problems get sorted out sooner or later!*

*Also we are both perfectionists. Sometimes we have to
compromise. Some problems are about us trying to make
everything perfect, when something less would be good
enough. For example, we ordered envelopes for our cards,
and they were a tiny bit too big. We wanted to get rid of
them, but we asked some other people and they didn't
agree that it was a problem. So we kept them and are
using them. Everyone seems happy, so really it was just a
problem in our eyes.*

4. So are you getting better at solving problems?

    *Definitely! We are better at identifying them, fixing them,
    and better at not getting pulled off track when they occur.*

Questions to Ask Yourself

- Am I keeping going in spite of any problems I encounter?
- Have I learned anything so far?
- Am I getting better at responding to and dealing with problems?
- Have I improved my approach to my dream in any way? Have I updated my map?
- Do I feel confident about what's next? Why?
- What can I do to make me feel even more confident?

Summary

Problems are inevitable on any worthwhile and complex activity like achieving a dream. Finding problems should not be seen as a reason to stop, but instead as a sign that you are making progress. The most successful people also have problems – their skill is not avoiding problems, but overcoming them.

Of course, you should try to minimize the problems you will hit, by thinking them through and working ways around them when drawing your map – and by identifying things that will increase your chances of success. However, even the best thinking will not avoid all problems. Resolve problems by calmly thinking them through and working out the best way around them. Very few problems are truly insurmountable.

Never see problems as a reason to quit your dreams – but only as a reason to quit the wrong tactics.

7 LOOK FORWARD

Obstacles are those frightful things you see when you take your eyes off your goal.

Henry Ford

The Goal

An important factor in making progress is your ability to look forward and always keep your end goal in mind. When working on your dream, it is easy to get sidetracked by frequent interruptions, working on the less important things on your map, losing focus on the work at hand or the end goal.

These interruptions happen to everyone, no matter how disciplined or focused they generally are. We simply cannot be at our best every day of the week. That's why we want to share a few tips that will help you keep your focus on the right things and get you back on track when you find yourself sidetracked from making progress on your dream.

Deal with Interruptions

One of the most common problems in keeping focus is not being able to deal with interruptions. When we try to do the work we set out to do, we get interrupted by something or someone, lose precious time and end up not making meaningful progress on our dream. In some situations, interruptions are frequent and a major barrier to achieving success.

Interruptions can be both internal and external. Internal interruptions are those we generate through our own thoughts and emotions. They have an important negative impact on our focus, and how often and how fast we achieve our dreams. Occasionally, we interrupt ourselves because we are lazy, more often it is because we are unmotivated or even afraid to work on our dream. If you do not work on your dream for various reasons of your own making, do some self-analysis and ask yourself important questions, such as:

- What is the real obstacle stopping me from doing the work I should be doing? How can I overcome it?
- How do I feel about what I should be doing? Why?
- Should I be doing something different to achieve my dream than what I have thought about and drawn for myself?
- Do I really want to make *this* dream come true?

If you hesitate when answering these questions or find yourself unable to give clear answers, it may mean you have fooled yourself into trying to work on the wrong dream. It's not something you really want and it's not something that you are passionate about. You may need to change dream, or more positively improve the way you envision it. This is not a bad outcome if it means you are learning more about what you really want – and as long as it makes you choose the dream you really want!

External interruptions are those created by other people and by events we have little or no control over. Dealing with them is more straightforward than we often care to admit. It boils down to answering two questions:

- Is this really urgent?
- Is this important to me?

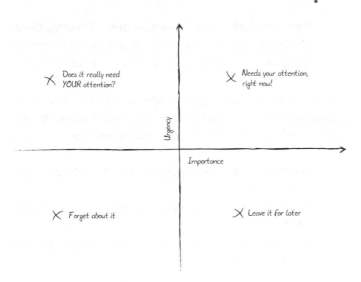

Depending on your answers, the strategy for dealing with them is simple:

- **Urgent and important interruptions need your attention now.** Go ahead and deal with them. However, make sure to find time to catch up on what you were supposed to do, as soon as possible. If other people are waiting on your work, don't forget to let them know about the delay, as soon as you can.
- **Urgent but unimportant interruptions might not need your specific attention.** Usually, somebody else can take care of them. Ask somebody else to deal with them and continue to work on your dream.
- **Non urgent but important interruptions can be handled at another time.** Schedule another day, time or place and take care of them. For now, focus on your dream and do the work you should be doing.

- **Non urgent and unimportant interruptions should not preoccupy you at all.** Simply focus on the work you should be doing and forget about them.

It is important to analyze your progress and how many interruptions you generally have to deal with. If you often encounter urgent and important interruptions, you should ask yourself:

- Are these real interruptions created by others, or are they created by myself?
- Am I just finding excuses not to do the work I should? Why?
- Am I generally choosing the wrong time or place to work on my dream?

Once you have dealt with interruptions, focus on your dream, what you do next and what you would like to achieve.

Quit the Unimportant

You may find that your map includes elements and steps that are not really important to achieving your dream. The clearest sign of this is that you find the time to work on your dream but, even if after you have done a lot of work, you do not make real progress. You are not feeling closer to achieving your dream. If you see this happening, then don't hesitate to analyze the map you have drawn so far. Take each element and the steps involved and ask yourself: *how does this contribute to making this dream come true?*

Most probably you will not be able to give clear answers for all of the items on your map. Only work on the items where you are able to clearly identify how doing that task takes you closer to making your dream come true. If you focus in this way, you will be positively surprised by the results you get.

Another important barrier to making real progress on your dream is managing your time and how much of it you use to work on your dream. If you regularly end up without the time to work on your dream, you need to stop and ask yourself:

- What occupies most of my time each day? Why?
- Can I do something to improve how much time I spend doing any of these things?
- Can I request help from other people for any of these things?
- What is really important out of all these things?
- What should I stop doing, so that I can make real progress on my dream?

Answering these questions truthfully will reveal interesting insights about what you should stop doing. Maybe you are doing too much overtime at your daily job and you have little time and energy left in the evenings to work on your dream. Maybe you are travelling or going out too much. Maybe you have family issues that require too much of your attention. Whatever it is, answer honestly and think about your true priorities. If something you are regularly spending time on is not important to you, consider stopping it. You don't have to do it abruptly, especially if it involves other people. Talk with them honestly about it and, together, find solutions that work both for you and them. Remember that quitting what's not important to you is much better than quitting your dream.

Another aspect we generally fail to consider is that we can ask for help and regularly receive it from others. Maybe you have too much on our plate at work and could ask your manager and colleagues for a bit of help. If you ask for help, often you will receive it.

Get Back on Track

When you read a compass, you must follow the bearing exactly so that you get to the destination you want. Even if you are only a few degrees off, by the time you have travelled many miles you will be far away from where you want to be. The same applies to your dream. Keep a constant eye on your map, evaluate your progress and understand where you are in your adventure towards making the dream come true.

If you notice that you have become derailed from the path to your goal and are going in a different direction, it is time to stop and understand what is going on:

- How far off are you, relative to the map you created?
- What are the reasons for this?
- Is this taking you in a good direction towards your dream?
- What do you need to change from now on? Is it some detail about your dream, the map or what you are doing to accomplish the dream?

In your daily job, you might have a manager or colleague always keeping you on your toes, making sure you are going in the right direction. When it comes to your dreams though, usually there isn't anyone else except you to keep yourself on track. So, make sure you evaluate your progress regularly and, when you notice getting yourself side-tracked, make the required changes to get back on track.

If you are bad at keeping yourself on track, then ask for help from someone you trust: a close friend, your partner, your parents, etc. Arrange for regular discussions with that person about your dream. During each discussion, cover important elements such as: the work you have recently done on your dream, where you believe you are now versus the destination, the problems you have encountered, what you have learned and what you plan to do next. Listen to what they say in response. You will find this exercise to be powerful, as:

- It forces you to evaluate your progress in a more honest way.
- Discussing your work with someone else reveals insights you might not notice.
- Having somebody else to regularly ask about your progress motivates you to work and make progress, which you can brag about the next time you meet.

If it feels weird to make an "official evaluation meeting", simply schedule it as something casual, but do it regularly. For example, one way that works for us is to schedule a long lunch with a close friend every two weeks or so. Even though we talk about many topics, we always bring the dream we are working on into the conversation. Most times, the other person becomes so engaged with what we're doing that they ask perceptive questions about our dream and constructively challenge the progress we are making.

There is one important thing to consider though: when you choose the person to talk to about your dream, pick someone who can relate to your dream and what you are doing. If the other person cannot understand your goal, actions and motivations, this will not be helpful.

Be Focused

Being focused is great for making meaningful progress but, unfortunately, it is not that easy to achieve. Focusing on achieving your dreams has two important dimensions:

- Being focused on the work you do to accomplish your dream.
- Believing in your dream at all times.

Let's start with being focused when doing the work. While focus is achieved differently from person to person, there are a few principles that always help:

- Work at a time when you are less likely to get distracted by others. For example, if mornings tend to be hectic, then work after lunch or during the evening, when things tend to be quieter and easier to manage.
- Work in spaces where you are less likely to get distracted from your work. Find places where you have both the balance and the tools you need. Depending on your dream, you might go for: a silent room, a library, your home desk, your garage, etc.
- Stay away from gadgets and devices that are likely to distract or interrupt you, unless they are needed in the work you do. Turning off your phone, or simply making it silent while you work, contributes a lot to becoming focused as soon as possible, for as long as possible. If

you work on your computer, close all your social net-
works, messaging tools, e-mail and any other application that is not useful in your work and likely to distract
you.

If you do get interruptions, look back over our recommendations for dealing with them. If you still don't feel focused and
you are not really working, consider doing the self-analysis we
advised in the first half of this chapter.

Believe in Your Dream

Being focused on your dream is all about keeping your faith
that you will succeed. No matter how fast or how slow progress
is, always keep your eyes on the end goal.

When you encounter problems, think about how your life will
be once your dream comes true. This will give you the positive
energy boost needed to help deal with problems. When things
are going well, do your best not to get side-tracked. If you do,
stop and get back on track. We shared some valuable tips for
doing so a little earlier in the chapter.

It may happen that you are working on what others think of
as a crazy or impossible dream, with no chance of success. If
that's the case for you, then remember Apple Computer's
"Think Different" campaign from 1997, which said: *". . . The
people who are crazy enough to think they can change the
world, are the ones who do."* (We recommend searching for it
on YouTube and viewing it a couple of times. It will energize
you and help get your belief back.)

Whatever you do, keep going and believe in your dream.

How will I Know I've Done Well?

The best indicator that you have the right amount of focus on your dream and end goals is your confidence level coupled with the amount of progress you make. Here are a few signs that you are doing well:

- **You are pleased with the amount of time you dedicate to working on your dream.** Only you can decide if you are spending the right amount of time. If you are not making progress and are constantly frustrated, you must face the challenge of finding more time and avoiding interruptions.
- **You feel that you have made some good progress** and you are getting closer to achieving your dream. Step-by-step it is getting closer.
- **You are passionately talking about your dream** and the next steps you'll take. Real belief in a dream is a powerful motivator to keep you going.
- **The people who help you are contributing to the dream as agreed.** They are focusing on the right things and they display energy and passion too.

What Our Heroes Say

Alex

This time we met with Alex in his team's research lab. It was fun to be surrounded by computers, scanners, microscopes and all kinds of research equipment. Research labs look just like they do in the movies: everything is white, the rooms are very well lit, clean and with lots of high tech equipment.

1. How are things going with your research? Where are you today?

   It's all good. Our grant proposal was approved and we received the resources required, even though there were some logistical delays. Unfortunately not all the research materials arrived on time. But we were able to work on other things than what we planned initially so we made some progress while the logistical issues were resolved.

   Fortunately for us, we got around the initial resourcing issues and our research has been underway for quite some time now. The results we have so far continue to be encouraging.

2. That is great news indeed. I imagine you have to deal with plenty of interruptions. Is that right?

   Yes, there are plenty of interruptions to deal with each day. The main source of interruptions is my phone. The device is both a blessing and a curse. I love that it allows me to get in touch with people and solve problems, but there are times when it really distracts me from doing real work. It often happens that I receive phone calls during a research experiment and I have to deal with it somehow, as I cannot afford to shut down the phone entirely, so that I can focus on my work.

Another source of interruptions is new deadlines that come up in my daily classes at the university. Quite a few professors change their mind about an exam or a paper and this impacts the amount of time I can dedicate to my research. Also, the committee which we need to submit regular reports to about the progress of our research work has a habit of changing deadlines with little advance notice.

3. How do you deal with these interruptions?

It is tricky, especially when it comes to my phone being the source of interruptions. Let's assume I am working on a research experiment and my phone rings. If I am called by someone from the research team, then I do my best to pick up and make myself available as soon as I can. If it is someone else, most times I simply do not take the call.

If there is a team mate working with me and I need to answer the phone, I ask him or her to take over and continue what I was doing while I answer the phone.

No matter how much I try to balance things, I end up not answering quite a few phone calls. So there are friends and family members who do not love me too much right now! The only solution I've found is to install an application on my phone, which keeps a log of my missed calls and allows me to set a reminder to call each person back when I have some time available.

4. What about the new deadlines showing up?

When that happens, I try to delegate more of my work to different team members who have more time available than

I do. This really works for me but I need to be careful not to overdo it and create problems within the team. Sometimes I simply cannot delegate to anyone and I take care of the deadline and postpone some of the work I need to do for our team's research.

5. Is it easy for you to focus on the work needed to accomplish your dream?

   If I work by myself or just with another person, I have no problem with that. However, when more members of our team are gathered together, it is easy for all of us to get side-tracked and do less valuable work. That's because we tend to share stories, facts or interesting things we've learned that are not necessarily related to our work.

6. How do you deal with this problem?

   It is not that easy. For us, it is important to get 2 to 3 hours of focused work per day in order to progress at the rhythm we want. We were working less than 2 hours together and that was not good. So we decided to start each meeting by talking and reviewing the main objectives of the day. We look at what we need to finish first, do those things, and then we allow ourselves to focus on other things. Most times it works but it can happen, every once in a while, that we get less work done than we would like to.

7. Have you found yourself going in a different direction than the one you set out initially?

   When working on any kind of research, getting side-tracked from the initial goal is very easy. You experiment and notice something that you weren't expecting. That gets your attention and you do more tests and experiments in that area. Then this gets noticed by other team members who continue your work, because your findings are unexpected and interesting. After a few days of work, you stop and realize you haven't made any real progress towards the initial goal and all these new tests and experiments have led you nowhere useful.

8. That's not a great place to be in. What do you do, to make sure you don't get too far from your initial goals?

    We learned that it helps to keep research logs. Each team member completes a summary of each experiment they work on and we review this log regularly. If we notice that the work we've done recently isn't taking us where we need to be, we stop working on the current experiments and postpone them until later, even though they seem awfully interesting. Then, we come back to our initial objectives and decide on what the most appropriate next steps are, so that we get back on track.

Olive

We catch up with Olive, and we are pleased to see her looking happy and relaxed, as she has managed to secure a new job and has managed to solve both of the problems we discussed in Persevere. We get the feeling that things must be going pretty well.

1. It's great to hear the good news that you've found a new job. What do you do?

   I am the manager (or coordinator if you would like) of a new business portal, that will soon be launched. It is a very ambitious project, aiming to bring a different perspective to how online business journalism is done in my country.

   It is a huge learning curve for me and, since I started, it has proved to be a very demanding position. However, I am optimistic that I will learn as I work on the project and do a good job in the end. It is funny that I am the youngest member of the team and yet I am the coordinator. It is a challenging position to find myself in.

2. Congratulations! What about your dream of becoming a bar singer?

   I've just resumed my canto lessons and in the last 2 weeks I've had two sessions with my teacher.

3. Any other good news to share?

   While talking with one of my oldest friends, he offered to help me out and have me join his young rock band, during their rehearsal sessions. Now I am attending most of their rehearsals and I sing along with them on cover songs they want to learn or improve. It's a win-win collaboration: I get to learn how to sing on stage with a whole band behind me, have fun and I also help them pay their rent for the rehearsal studio they are using.

4. Do you need to handle many interruptions when working on your dream?

I do have to handle some interruptions. For example, I was recording at home and my phone was ringing. Since I was waiting for phone calls about scheduling job interviews, I could not afford to turn off my phone while practising. Now that this is solved, I'm OK with muting my phone while practising.

I also have to deal with interruptions in the process of taking lessons. For example, with my canto teacher – I didn't get the chance to meet her for a while. Therefore, I had to rethink my practising and do it alone, at home, in order to still achieve some progress, even if she was not there to guide me.

5. Have you found yourself going in a different direction than the one you set out initially?

At some point, I noticed I was distracting myself from working on this dream, by letting myself get involved in a project of one of my friends, who wanted to build a cool website. I helped him out a bit with what he needed, but then I spent more time working on it and added elements and details to it, even though he didn't ask for them. In the end, I noticed that I had wasted a few days not working on my dream and decided to stop and get back to the work.

6. Is it easy for you to focus on the work needed to accomplish your dream?

Well, given the fact that my dream is not about "finding the lost land of Atlantis", it's quite easy for me to do so. It's a very pleasant activity. I sing when I am in the shower, I sing when I am cleaning, I sing when I go out with my friends in karaoke bars. My work is actually my way of relaxing after a day's activities. So yes, I find it easy to focus.

Of course, there are moments when I record the same song over and over again and I get angry or tired if it does not sound as well as it should. I'm lucky that does not happen very often.

7. Are you pleased with the amount of progress done so far?

    I would be lying if I said yes. However, there is a positive side to where I am at today: this time gap allowed me to meet the band I was talking about. This will help me a lot in the long run. All in all I'm not in a bad position. I have resumed my canto lessons, and I collaborate regularly with a young rock band. Now I actually have five people teaching me how to be a better singer. :)

8. Regarding the problems you encountered and your initial plans: how do they impact the time it will take for you to finish the work on your dream?

    It is not that easy to say with certainty. Most probably they will add 2 to 3 months to the total time I need until I sign a contract for professional singing. However, the recent developments have been very positive and I am more confident that I will pull this off. I was getting worried that I wouldn't solve my professional situation and would have to stop working on my dream for a while.

Anna and Amelia

Anna and Amelia shared the way they keep focused on the future – but we can't talk to them for too long, as right now this interview is the distraction stopping them progress!

1. Do you manage to keep focused on your end goal?

   Generally yes, but probably not as much as we should do or want to. Some days it goes really well and we make lots of progress. On other days there is interruption after interruption. Achieving our dream is always on our minds, but circumstances can be distracting.

2. What differentiates the good from the bad days?

   We have found we work better when we have very specific, very clear tasks to work on, with a fixed deadline. We were working to a series of externally set deadlines – we had to be ready for a trade show, or we had an order to complete for a customer. Now we set our own deadlines. Even if they are artificial, they really help to keep us focused and make progress.

3. Do you think short term or long term?

   Well both, but we need immediate goals to keep working on a daily basis, whilst really being conscious of what we are trying to achieve overall. We have a clear vision of operating a business with steady sales. We have some sales now, but not enough to sustain the business.

   To some extent it is still trial and error. We don't mean it's accidental, just that we are learning as we go along. We take small steps all the time, but we cannot be absolutely sure how many small steps make up the really big step of achieving our dream. The big picture is there, but at any one moment we are very focused on short term tasks and today's steps.

4. Are you still going where you originally dreamed?

   Oh yes! We have some other ideas in the background, which we will develop more when the current dream has really got going, or if it is not successful.

   The next event, which is a major craft show in the north of England, is really important for us. Depending on the volume of business we generate, we will either keep going or we will need to rethink our plans. That might be new products, different pricing, or different routes to market. We won't think too deeply about it until we know the outcome. For now we are focused on the original dream.

5. Do you have any tips for anyone else about how to keep going?

   - *Keep your big dream in your mind all the time.*
   - *Set deadlines to get things done – even if a deadline is not really necessary.*
   - *Set tighter deadlines than you think necessary for any third party or supplier who is doing anything for you. They are not all reliable and you need time to recover if they don't deliver.*
   - *Be realistic about how much you can do, and constantly willing to re-prioritize depending on how things work out in reality. Don't beat yourself up because you can only do a limited number of things in a day. Plan to do that limited number of things.*
   - *If you can delegate some of the work – do, but keep an eye on it!*

Questions to Ask Yourself

- Am I pleased with the amount of time I spend working on my dream?
- Am I managing to avoid internal and external interruptions?
- Am I effectively prioritizing those things I really need to do, and identifying those that can be left for later, dealt with by someone else or ignored?
- Do I feel like I am making meaningful progress while working?
- Is there anyone who can help me stay on track?
- Is the direction I'm heading taking me closer to achieving the dream? Am I staying on track?
- Do I believe that I will succeed in making the dream come true?

Summary

To reach your desired goal of making your dream a reality, you must keep this goal in mind all the time. It is easy to become sidetracked, bogged down in interruptions or to spend time on unimportant issues and irrelevant details. To avoid this you should keep looking forwards, in the direction set by your map, all the way to your end goal.

Most of us become side-tracked at some point or other. When this happens it is important to recognize it and get back on track. Life is full of interruptions – created by those around us or by ourselves. Focus your time on the important things, and prioritize the urgent. Everything else either can be left for later, dealt with by someone else or ignored. To help you stay on track, work at a time and in a place where you are less likely to get interrupted, keep believing in your dream and stay focused on your map.

8 ARRIVE

*There are two kinds of people,
those who finish what they start
and so on.*

Robert Byrne

The Goal

Arriving at the end of your dream is exciting. After so much work, overcoming problems, learning from mistakes, you've done it! Your dream has come true and it is time to stop and enjoy the achievement.

Unfortunately, it's not always easy to figure out when the dream has actually been achieved. That's why, in this chapter, we share some tips that will help to make sure you don't stop either too early or too late. We will also show you what to do once you have arrived, so that you enjoy your dream, learn from your adventure and thank the people who have helped you on your way.

When to STOP?

One of the important traits most successful people have is knowing when to stop working on a dream, so they can focus on the next one.

The ideal point to stop is when you have achieved the desired outcomes of your dream. You are now in the position you dreamt of being in. All the elements you have drawn on your map are in place and you are enjoying the benefits of making the dream come true.

People who don't know when to stop either stop too early, before the dream is fully achieved, or they stop too late, long after the initial dream has been achieved. Another bad scenario is when they never stop and keep adding more and more elements to their dream.

As you achieve more of your dreams, you will become better at identifying when they are done and when to stop working on them. But until you do, let's talk about some troublesome scenarios you could find yourself in:

- **Stopping too early** – people tend to stop working too early on a dream because they are not going deeply enough into the dream or because things did not go so well and fear took the lead. The best way to make sure you are not making this mistake is to look at your map and think about two very important questions we suggested at the beginning:
  - What must be in place for my dream to be reality?
  - So, what steps do I need to take, to put these things in place?

  Answer truthfully and see what is not yet in place for your dream to be complete. Even if there are only a few elements left, make sure you tend to them and get them done, no matter how hard it seems. There's no point in stopping now that you are so close to making your dream come true. If the reason for not getting everything done is a negative one and you have encountered problems that have made you stop, then go through the tips we shared in the Persevere chapter. They will help you overcome the problems and quit some of the wrong tactics you might have applied.

- **Stopping too late** – as shared in the Progress chapter, some people are guilty of being in love with the feeling of being busy. Therefore, they keep adding elements to their map endlessly, even though they have achieved what they initially set out to do. This is not a good way forward. Take some time to analyze what you are doing and answer the following questions:

- Have you achieved the dream you initially set out to do and all its important elements?
- Are you in the habit of adding more elements to your map, each time you evaluate it and achieve some of the things you have drawn on it?
- What is the reason for adding elements on a continuous basis?

If you keep adding new and better dimensions to your dream, you should STOP. Enjoy your achievement, internalize the important lessons you've learned and then start working on a new dream, which builds on the one you just achieved. Simply adding new elements to a dream which is already achieved is not an ideal way forward. You don't get to enjoy your success, you do not have a feeling of achievement and you do not get the chance to internalize important lessons you've learned along the way. Applying this strategy won't make you better at achieving future dreams.

Now that you have achieved the dream you set out to accomplish and all the elements are in place, it is time to stop and learn.

Learn

The best way to learn is to spend some time thinking about your adventure. Reserve at least a few hours for this process, if not a few days, especially for the most important dreams you have achieved.

Have the maps you have drawn at hand. If you created multiple versions, place them all in front of you and look at how they have changed. Then, answer these questions:

- Which were the elements on your initial map?
- What changed along the way?
- What were the reasons for each important change?
- What can you learn from each change?
- What went wrong?
- Why did things go wrong?
- What will you change on my next dream?
- What went fantastically well?
- Why did they go well?
- What should you keep doing, from all the things that worked well?
- Is there anything you did not do, that you will do next time?
- How will this make your next dream even better?

Most probably you worked on your dream with other people. To maximize your learning you should ask them these questions too. Spend some time with the people who helped along the way and discuss these questions. The discussions will reveal important lessons you won't identify by yourself.

One of the mistakes we tend to make at this point is to focus our thinking and discussions mostly on the things that did not work well. This tactic is not constructive and, if some things went badly wrong, it can easily turn into a fight or a blame game. Don't do that to yourself and others. It will only ruin your enjoyment of the achievement, without learning anything new and valuable. Instead, do your best to think and discuss more the things that went well – and even fantastically well! We are sure you'll find that you did many things well. Focus on them and learn more about what you did and how it led to great results.

Make sure you keep this learning in mind and apply it to your future dreams. Learning more about your real strengths is a lot more useful than learning about your weaknesses. Use this learning when you think about your next dream and draw the map of your next adventure.

Pay Your Debts

Once we achieve something, we are often in a rush to get to the next dream. We barely take the time to stop and pay our debts to others. When we say debts, we are not just thinking of the financial implications of this word.

Obviously, you should pay any money you may owe to others for accomplishing your dream. However, you surely accumulated more than just financial debt. Consider debts of the more personal kind: acknowledging the people who helped you, saying thank you to those who deserve it, helping them with something that matters to them or giving them a small gift, as a token of your appreciation.

Whatever you do, do not forget about this important aspect. It will build a very positive karma that benefits everybody involved:

- First, it makes you feel good about yourself and your achievement.
- It makes others feel good and rewarded for helping you.
- Your relationship will become stronger and you are more likely to help each other in the future.

Celebrate

Last, but not least, don't forget to celebrate and enjoy your achievement. It helps to celebrate in a bigger way than you would normally, involving people you enjoy spending time with. Don't hesitate to do something you don't generally do:

- Go out to a fancy restaurant or some crazy club.
- Take a vacation and enjoy yourself.
- Take some time off and do more of the things you enjoy doing.
- Buy yourself that cool gadget you set your heart on.

Be creative about your celebration ideas. Go for it! What sense is there in achieving your dreams if you don't celebrate them?

How will I Know If I've Done Well?

Let's recap the signs that show you are done:

- **You are satisfied with where you have arrived.** All the important elements of your dream are in place and you have achieved the outcome you were dreaming of. You feel a sense of achievement and excitement about the end result.
- **You have learnt valuable lessons.** You feel that you are a better person, who has learned important lessons during this adventure. You are more aware of your strengths and weaknesses and plan to use more of your strengths in the future.

- **You feel lucky and grateful for the help you received.** Now that your dream has come true, you are both happy and grateful for having great people to help you. You are sharing your achievement with others and you are thinking of good ways to thank them and return the favour in a way that is meaningful to them.
- **You may feel something is missing.** Some people quickly start to miss the buzz and energy of working on their dream. If you feel this – it's time to move on to the next one!

What Our Heroes Say

Alex

We meet Alex close to the research lab. He is looking calm and happy when we start our interview. You can tell he has been working hard, but there is a sparkle in his eye as he talks to us.

1. Have you finished the work on your dream?

   Not yet but we are awfully close. The research is finished, the research thesis is almost done and we are working on scheduling the review with the official evaluation committee. Three more weeks and we're done. :)

2. That sounds great. Are you confident that everything will work well until the very end?

   Yes. The hard work is behind us now and the results we have obtained are very exciting. I don't think we will have problems convincing the committee about the quality of our work and the relevance of the results we have.

3. Are you sure you have stopped working on your research at the right time?

   Well . . . I don't think we are in danger of having stopped too early. If we had done that, we would have had a very thin research paper with weak claims and less documented proof than we do today. Also, I don't think our senior investigator would have given his sign off on it.

It is more likely that we stopped a bit late and worked more than needed. However, I can't think of a good way to identify when you are doing that, at least not when it comes to research work. It simply feels right. We all have a feeling of closure and we are anxious about the final steps.

4. How do you feel, now that you are so close to making this dream come true?

I'm both happy and tired. I know I am not completely off the hook yet. There are a few weeks left but I already have a feeling of relief. This adventure is going to end soon and I will be in the position I dreamt of being in.

It was a very complex dream to manage, the biggest I've had so far. However, I really feel I've achieved something worthwhile and I can't wait to be in front of the evaluation committee and talk with them about our team's work.

5. What are the main lessons you've learned while working on this dream?

I have not had much time to meditate on this so far, since we are not fully done with our work. However, I can quickly think of three very important lessons:

- *It was great that I spent some quality time together with the initial research team, to identify a good senior investigator to sponsor us. His help was crucial to our success. For example, he used his network when we needed some funds to finish our preliminary research. He also coached me and the rest of the team when needed, and showed us better ways to work or shared ideas that helped solve certain problems.*

- *I've learned that it is great to establish a very diverse research team. In our final team we had people with different backgrounds, seniorities and working styles. We learned a lot from each other and we have improved a lot as a group. If you evaluate us today, we are much better professionals than when we started working together.*

- *Creating some rules about the way we worked as a team helped a lot in establishing a predictable rhythm to our work. It helped to have a regular weekly team meeting and to create a research log with the things each person was working on. Last but not least, it was very useful to use the whiteboard in our research lab, to keep everyone updated with the latest status notes and the next steps we are supposed to be working on.*

6. How do you plan to celebrate once everything is done?

I simply want to take some time off and go somewhere far from the research lab. I don't want to use any phones, computers or research equipment for a few days. I just want a quiet place, in the middle of nature. I want to wake up at lunch time, relax and enjoy a few slow paced days, without much going on.

All in all, it's a great feeling to be here right now. And it is going to be even better when I come back from a little vacation. But I'm aware that, in a sense, this is just the beginning. I need this degree to "break the ice" and enter the scientific community. There is still lots to be done.

Olive

We meet Olive in a smart and friendly cafe not far from where she lives. We all order a coffee before we get down to talking.

1. Have you finished the work on your dream?

   Not yet but I am close. I am working on the last important element of my dream: getting a contract as a singer. I have recorded some demo tapes and have had discussions with several bar managers and PR coordinators I know from a previous job. I also shared the demo tapes with most of them.

2. How did the discussions go?

   Overall, I think they went well. There are many bars that have themed events that take place once every few months or once a month. The agreement I made with most of the people I talked to was for them to call me when they plan to organize such events. The pay is really poor for these small singing gigs and there is not a lot of competition. This should increase my chances of success as earning money from singing is not an important factor for me at this moment.

   Some even promised to call and give me a shot before posting any job ads or spreading the word to others, which is great.

3. That sounds good. How long do you think it will take until you get called to sing for your first event?

   It shouldn't take long. I should be able to have my first official "concert" within the next 2 months. I've talked with people who own bars that have a blues or jazz night once a month and with others who have themed events for different celebrations: Halloween, Valentine's Day, etc. I should be able to sing soon at this kind of event.

4. But these are temporary events. How long you still have to go until you get a long-term contract for a regular collaboration?

I've learned that occasional concerts can transform into long term collaborations. It is important for me to perform my best during the first collaborations so that the audience enjoys my singing and the bar owners are happy. If I can pull this off, it should not take me more than 6 months until a bar offers me a contract for a regular, long-term collaboration.

5. How did you manage to reach the people you have had these discussions with?

That was easy. A few months before we started our conversation, I was working in my spare time as a reporter and photographer for a website that covered concerts and other cultural events. Therefore I went to many concerts, in lots of places and met with a lot of people working in this field. I had quite a big list of contacts to talk to about what I want to do.

6. How do you plan to make sure you stop working on your dream at the right time?

I will "stop" only when I have the long term contract I want. Until then, I need to keep working at it. I don't think I am in danger of stopping too early or too late. I will have become a good bar singer when someone considers me worthy of signing a long term contract with them.

7. What are the main lessons you've learned while working on this dream?

Good question! I've learned quite a few things so far. I think the most important are:

1. *When you work on a dream that is not major, in the sense that your life does not depend on it, chances are that everything else in your life becomes a priority and stops you from moving further forward. It happened to me when I decided to quit my job and focus on finding a new one. I almost stopped working on this dream and the only way I could move forward was by trying to be more disciplined. If you work on a similar dream, be honest with yourself and make sure you really do your best to keep things on track. Otherwise, it won't happen.*

2. *When I work on my next dream, I want to talk more openly about it. I've learned that, when people hear you talking about your dreams, they actually listen. If they relate to your dreams, they will help. I thought about this dream for many years and but I only started working on it after I talked about it with others. If I had not spoken about it with my canto teacher, she wouldn't have offered to help and I wouldn't be here today, so close to making it happen. It is so much easier to keep going when others know about your dream, ask you about it and give you a hand when you need it. Don't keep your dreams hidden under the blanket, like I did. Dare to talk about them openly. Otherwise, you might never start working on them.*

3. *Last but not least, if a dream is important, expect that you will need to make trade-offs and give certain*

things up. For example, I enjoy smoking but I now do it less than I used to, because it helps with my voice. If I know that I have to sing in a rehearsal or a demo recording later, I don't drink any kind of alcohol, not even a glass of really good wine.

8. Thanks for sharing these lessons. How do you plan to celebrate once everything is done?

The moment I will have signed a long term contract, the celebration will be my first concert as part of that deal. I will invite all my friends and make sure they are there to hear me sing. The performance itself will be my celebration and I plan to enjoy every moment of it.

Amelia and Anna

We meet Amelia and Anna late one evening. They have returned from their second trade show. When we arrive their car is still full of their display stand and samples. They are tired after a long day followed by a long drive, but both seem excited. First we help them unpack before asking our questions.

1. How did it go?

   The show went really well. It was a big thing for us. We are both very pleased. We met lots of potential clients, got some good leads from people who are interested in stocking and selling our work and also made some actual sales at the show. It wasn't perfect, but we are learning to treat the things that go wrong as opportunities to learn.

2. So, have you now completed your dream?

   Well yes and no! Yes, because we have achieved the basic part of our dream – to get our business up and running. We can really say it now exists. No, because we now have the work to do to turn it into a long term successful business. On balance and in the context of what we set out to do, we think the best way to put it is that we have finished the first stage, and that was what our dream was about.

3. Do you think you will keep going now?

   Oh yes! Why wouldn't we? There is lots more to do and plenty to keep us busy. Working on our dream in a structured way got us somewhere we really wanted to get to. Probably both of us, deep down, were unsure if we would be able to pull it off this far. We have a real business now. It is small, but growing it will be more straightforward than starting it in the first place.

4. Have you learnt much along the way?

There are lots of things about the business we didn't know. We were probably a little naive, but you have to start somewhere and no-one knows everything. On top of that, we have learnt about ourselves, both individually and working as a pair. Not everything we did together worked well – but we have really learnt how to use each other's strengths and weaknesses.

And then of course, we have learnt much more about how to get things done. There are lots of things we could pick on. Most important is probably having a clear vision of what we wanted to achieve together with a level of flexibility. You have to be flexible, all sorts of things arose that we did not expect: some to do with the business, and some to do with other things in our lives which just got in the way. The secret seems to be finding that balance between being driven, but also knowing when to do something differently from what you originally planned.

Another thing we would advise anyone who is doing something they haven't done before is to constantly experiment. Don't spend forever thinking – try some stuff. If it works, great. But it's great if it doesn't work as well, as long as you learn and then adjust what you are doing. The most important thing is to take action and make some progress.

Finally, there are lots of people out there who have done something similar, and most of them are willing to help and give advice if you just ask.

5. What now then?

Right now? Probably a quick glass of wine and then a long, long sleep, before picking up and driving the business forward tomorrow.

Questions to Ask Yourself

- Am I stopping at the right moment – neither too soon nor too early?
- Are all the elements on my map completed?
- Have I achieved the outcome I desired from this dream?
- What are the lessons I have learned?
- Have I paid my debts to others?
- Have I celebrated achieving this dream?

Summary

After all your hard work you will achieve your dream. To do this, you must identify when it is time to stop – neither stopping too early when there are still important things to do, nor stopping too late by constantly playing around with irrelevant details.

If you stop too late you are not taking time to enjoy the dream. Go on – live it! Additionally, you are avoiding making yourself free to achieve your next dream.

Before you move on, thank all the people who helped you achieve your dream and have a celebration. Then, having achieved a dream, you are ready to move on to the next one. To be even better next time, take the time to consider the whole experience of making your dream reality. Think through what went well and what went badly so you learn and improve your approach to making all your future dreams reality.

9 DREAM SOME MORE

We grow great by dreams. All big men are dreamers.

Woodrow Wilson

The Goal

Right back at the start of this book, when we began on the journey of achieving a dream, we asked you to focus on *one* dream. We asked that, because we believe that through focus you achieve more in life. But we know you have got many more dreams, and now is the time to take them out from the store-rooms in your mind and think about what happens next.

What we have described in this book is not just a linear process. We see it as an ongoing cycle. It is a cycle that starts repeatedly with new dreams whenever an old dream is fulfilled. The completion of one cycle triggers the start of the next. Our goal in this book is to help you not just achieve a dream, but all of your dreams.

You might ask, why? What is the goal of all of this? At one level it is simply about getting things done, achieving the things you want to achieve and becoming the person you want to become. Yet there is a deeper truth. We have not set out to write a philosophy book or a book on positive thinking, but there is an element of this underlying our approach. The real goal of achieving your dreams is to find your own happiness and to grow great, in terms of what happiness and greatness mean to you personally.

Reflect on Where You Have Come from

We are not great believers in looking backwards. The most value in life comes from thinking about the future and looking to where you are going. But sometimes, especially when you have completed something great, like achieving one of your dreams, looking backwards for a short period can be very powerful.

Look back, see how far you have come, see how much you have learnt and how much you have achieved in your life so far. Think about the dream you have completed, and then think about all the other things you have managed to do. Feel good about yourself. Feel *really* good about yourself. Happiness is a powerful motivator to future success. More importantly, it is a justified reward in itself.

Reflect on What You Have Learned

One of the most important things in completing a dream is how it sets you up for achieving the next one. We all benefit from advice and help. But the best teachers are usually ourselves. The simple approach of doing things and then reflecting on how they went and what you can learn from the experience of undertaking activities is extremely powerful. Since the earliest days, mankind has learnt from personal experience.

We all learn from our experiences, but the most effective learning comes from consciously reflecting on those experiences and deciding how you will use the lessons learnt in future. Unless you really do things differently, you will get exactly the same results. In Arrive, we posed some questions to help you learn about *how* to approach your next dream. Now we want you to do something different. We want you to think about *where* your dreams are taking you.

Important as it is to have and achieve dreams, each dream is just a step in your journey. Each step will be different: some will be very important to you, others will be a small movement forward; some steps will be easy whereas others will be challenging; some will be successful whilst a few will not. On your journey each step counts, but the accumulation of steps is much more important.

For a while, we would suggest a few days, step back from thinking about individual dreams and think more broadly. Try to form a mental picture of the dreams that you keep coming back to:

- Has this picture changed since you started out on the dream you have just completed – is that a change you welcome or resist?
- What are the most important things in life for you?
- Will the dreams you have help you to achieve those things – or should you have different dreams?
- Are you becoming the person you want to become?

People who achieve a lot tend to have many dreams. Thinking of one dream often encourages thinking about others. For a limited period of time, we want you to let all the different dreams play out in your mind and to think deeply about whom you want to be and what your journey in life is.

Once you have done this for a short while, you will be ready to start to focus again and think about exactly which dream you are going to pursue next. What we want you to avoid is automatically following a defined list of dreams. We want you to work on the dreams that really should be most important to you. Consider:

- The life journey you want to take and the best way to travel.
- What you know about yourself, how you work best, what motivates you and what you enjoy doing.

- What you have learnt on the dreams you have completed.
- The resources you have access to: your time, money, other people's help, etc. – that will enable you to achieve your next dream.

Then decide.

Your next dream may be the second on your list of dreams when you started out. If so, that is great. But more often than not, we find that in the process of achieving your dreams, by the activities of working, thinking and learning, your list of dreams evolves. It changes and grows. Some old dreams may now seem stale – and there will be exciting new possibilities you didn't think of originally.

Making the decision on which dream comes next can be hard. This is an important decision, as you want to spend your life achieving your most important dreams. But no-one is perfect at making such decisions. Therefore, don't make the dream selection too stressful. If you really cannot decide – just choose one. After all, you will be able to come back and choose another dream next time.

Look Forward and Dream Some More

Start the next cycle when you are ready.

We all need to rest at times and, by all means, take a little break. After all, you have worked intensely to achieve your dream. But don't make the break too long. We are not suggesting that you constantly work hard, but we are suggesting that at no time should you have no dreams being progressed, even if that progression is slow to start with. We like the old saying "a change is as good as a rest".

So, start the cycle again. Follow the advice we gave in the Dream chapter, plus anything new you want to add. Everyone can build on and extend the advice we have given.

Go gently at first, until you are certain of your direction. And then move on with more urgency, when you are clear about your dream, especially if you find that sense of excitement that is typical when a great dream takes hold of you.

Get into the habit of dreaming, thinking, drawing and doing. As we said at the start of this chapter this is not because we believe that achieving lots of things is in itself important, but that through striving, learning and achieving we can attain fulfilment and happiness.

How will I Know If I've Done Well?

The most important way of deciding if you have done well, is to feel the sense that you are ready to move onto the next dream. It may have challenges and uncertainties, but then so do all valuable dreams. But you are prepared to start working your way through them.

Let's recap the signs that show you are done:

- **You have reflected and understood what you will build on** and what you will do differently in your next dream.
- **You are ready to start again** and you have that sense of drive and excitement that comes with a really appealing dream. The dream is important to you and important to achieving what you want in life.

- **You have an increased sense of confidence** about taking on challenging dreams.
- **You can improve on the ideas we have laid out in this book**. You are not only going on to your next dream – you are an experienced dream achiever. This time it will be even better!

What Our Heroes Say

Alex

It's our last meeting with Alex. We want to discuss what happens now, and how he will face his next dream.

1. When we started our conversation, you mentioned that one of your biggest dreams is to become a Physician Scientist. Has this dream changed since we first talked?

   No, it hasn't. Now I am in a better position to achieve this "ultimate" dream of mine, if it's OK to call it that.

2. Have you decided on what's next for you?

   Getting a doctoral degree has allowed me to work on the "Scientist" part of my dream. Now I need to focus on the "Physician" side of things. This means continuing my medical education with a focus on the practical medical skills, instead of the research ones. I will work on obtaining a Doctor of Medicine (MD) degree, which will mean going through some practical medical rotations, passing some important exams and so on.

   However, I don't plan to ignore the research side of things. I want to get myself involved in other research projects but not as a team coordinator. I want to be a coach, helping other students achieve dreams similar to the one I have just made come true for myself.

3. Do you feel more confident than you were when starting the work on this dream?

Definitely! I've gained an official status that puts me in a better position than before. Due to this, there are different and better opportunities available to me. Also, I have learned a lot in the process and I know what I want to do differently the next time I work on a similar dream.

4.   Speaking of that, what will you do differently when working on future dreams?

There is one big thing I want to change about my approach. I will no longer assume that, if I am excited about working on a dream that I believe is important, others will be too.

I want to work more on making sure people really understand the dream I'm asking for their help on. I want to do a better job at sharing the end goal, the benefits of us working together and my expectations of them. Also, I want to make sure I have a better understanding of their expectations from me and the dream we will be working on.

5.   That is a valuable lesson. Now that you are done with this dream, are you ready to start working on the next one?

Yes, I am!

Olive

We met with Olive a few weeks after our last conversation. As soon as we saw her, we noticed there was something different about her: she was very happy, energetic and we had the feeling she wanted to share something special with us.

1. Hey Olive! Do you have more updates to share with us since we last talked?

    Yes! It's brilliant to be able to share this: I succeeded! My dream has come true. One of my friends is opening up a bar this autumn. He heard me singing and asked me to sing there once a week. And I will have a long-term contract and everything.

2. That's awesome. Congratulations! We don't want to spoil your enjoyment of this moment but, have you decided on what's next for you?

    Besides rehearsing like a madwoman? I plan to enjoy being a bar singer for a while, see how it works out and how my professional career evolves in parallel with my singing.

    If I think about it, I might choose to work on another old dream of mine: opening my own coffee shop. I feel more at ease when working on my personal dreams now. Even if this will be a different kind of adventure, I think I can pull it off. However, I will need to work on it for a couple of years and raise the money required to open the coffee shop. That will be a big challenge.

3. What will you do differently when working on future dreams?

I want to stop dreaming and thinking about my dream without daring to take immediate action. To achieve this, I plan to:

- *Stop listening to people who are in the habit of saying that I cannot achieve certain things, even if they are close family members who are very dear to me.*
- *I will talk more about my dreams with people I appreciate. I feel that I now have more courage to say: "I want to do this, will you help me?"*

4. Do you feel more confident than you were when starting the work on this dream?

Oh . . . yes! The trip I went through made a huge difference to me. This is the first important personal dream I've worked on in my adult life. Now I feel more courageous about taking action than I used to. My fears are no longer as strong as they used to be.

Anna and Amelia

It's a wet and cloudy day when we catch up with Anna and Amelia in Amelia's house. They have come a long way and look happy when we start to discuss what happens next for them.

1. So where do you go from here?

   Anna: *Well, the main thing is to keep capitalizing on the investment we have made so far, both time and money, and building on our success to date.*

2. And longer term?

   Anna: *I think we will focus on building up the relationship with our customers. Our goal is not to have a product for everyone, but a product that appeals to a reliable set of regular customers. We think these customers will mostly be galleries and high end gift shops who stock handmade cards and prints.*
   Amelia: *We have more and more ideas for other products, but for now we will stay focused on the current designs. We will probably spend more time trying to sell the prints than the cards, because the margin is so much higher, but then again it's easier to sell cards.*
   Anna: *Yes, and then longer term, once we have a successful track record we will add more and more products. Ironically, we will do this if the current products continue to be successful – as then there is demand for our range. But, we will also do it if they stop being successful as then we need to find another way of making money!*

3. Have you enjoyed the experience?

   Amelia: *It's been great. I've never done anything like this in my life before and I have had a lot of fun. I really feel I've achieved something and it's a wonderful feeling.*

Anna: The best thing has been getting good feedback and seeing people excited or enthusiastic about our products. It's really rewarding. A trade show is very, very tiring, but it's worth it when you get that direct face-to-face feedback from a customer. One person saying a print is beautiful is just fantastic.

4. And what lessons have you taken for any dreams you pursue in future, or for other dreamers?

   Anna: You really have to believe in what you are doing. You have to be patient as things don't happen overnight. You need to be flexible. It's great to have a vision, but if you make it too precise you will cause trouble for yourself. You must have a sense of direction, but things will happen, which will make you want to flex it as you go along.

   Also accept that some of the work will be boring. This is when you need to keep sight of your dream. It's easy when it's exciting, but much harder on those days when it is dull. But the mundane stuff must get done as well. So when you need to do it, keep remembering the dream. You must find ways to rekindle the excitement all the time. It really helps to have two of us, as when either of us is a bit down, the other will push and keep the enthusiasm going.
   Amelia: My lesson is simpler. If you have a dream, START! Just get on and give it a go. Don't prevaricate; don't just keep talking about it. Yes, think and map it out, but most importantly do something.

5. Thanks for your insights, we've really enjoyed following your dream so far.

Questions to Ask Yourself

- How have my dreams changed from those I originally had?
- Am I better prepared for my next dream than I was for the first?
- Am I happier now that I have achieved my dream?
- If I achieved some more of my dreams, would I be happier still?
- Am I feeling energized and excited about the next adventure?
- When will I start thinking about what I am going to do next?

Summary

You have achieved your dream, and so now is the time to decide what comes next. Hopefully, one part of what comes next is to start working on your next dream – using everything you have learnt to achieve this dream to make the next dream even better. But the good life is not just concerned with achieving dreams, the good life is concerned with living. You have achieved a dream, so take the time to enjoy it.

We believe the way to a good life is to *dream* good dreams, to *do* good dreams and to *live* good dreams in an ongoing cycle. Go on, you can Dream it, Do it, Live it!

DRAWING MAPS WITH MIND MAPPING SOFTWARE

The approach used in the Draw chapter is based on developing a Mind Map. Mind Mapping is a technique that was developed by Tony Buzan. In fact, the name *Mind Map* was created by him. Buzan has been a long term evangelist for Mind Maps. He has spoken about, developed tools for and written extensively about Mind Maps. For example see:

- *How to Mind Map: The Ultimate Thinking Tool That Will Change Your Life*
- *The Mind Map Book: Unlock Your Creativity, Boost Your Memory, Change Your Life*

Both are by Tony Buzan.

We are really big fans of Mind Maps. We like the way they enable you to capture what can seem like unstructured thoughts and present them in an intelligible fashion. Unlike other techniques, such as writing lists, Mind Maps seem much more aligned with the way our brains works. They are great both for letting yourself explore a new topic in a creative freewheeling fashion, as well as structuring complex things you have thought long and hard about into action plans.

The instructions in the Draw chapter are enough to get you started with Mind Mapping, but getting the most from Mind Maps takes a little practice. This practice is about finding out what works best for you, rather than trying to learn some standard universal approach. You can read lots on Mind Maps. If you are the sort of person who likes to study something then go and do some reading. But our advice is to just give it a go. Mind mapping is really intuitive – that's what is great about it. Start with a blank sheet of paper, a topic you want to develop a Mind Map about and go!

However, you may find that if you really like Mind Mapping as much as we do that working with paper and pencil soon becomes onerous. You will want to regularly change and enhance your Mind Map, and often this requires redrawing. This activity is important, as the steps of tweaking and enhancing a Mind Map are all part of the creative process. But this constant re-drawing can become a chore. So, it may be better to consider Mind Mapping software which will redraw the Mind Map automatically as you add, amend or delete information.

There is a variety of Mind Mapping software available. Some is free, and we suggest you start with one of the free packages. However, we have to admit that some of the best have a price. Here are some suggestions:

- **XMind** – This comes in both a free and professional version with a charge.
  http://www.xmind.net
- **FreeMind** – An open source Mind Mapping packages.
  http://sourceforge.net/projects/freemind
- **iMindMap** – This is Tony Buzan's own product.
  http://www.thinkbuzan.com
- **Mindjet MindManager** – This is our favourite, as it is flexible and functionally rich. It is relatively expensive, but worth it if you find yourself Mind Mapping a lot.
  http://www.mindjet.com

ABOUT THE AUTHORS

Richard Newton I am a 48-year-old from the UK, with lots of experience in different areas – I am a project manager, a management consultant, a company director and author, but I would prefer not to be defined by that alone. I have achieved some of my dreams, in all sorts of different areas, but I have lots and lots more! I have two specific ambitions to achieve before I am 50 which I am working on right now. My consulting work takes me all around the world, mostly helping large companies with business and organizational change, or helping them to improve the ways they deliver projects and change. As an author I have published 9 books so far, which have been translated into 14 languages. They are all business and management books, but increasingly I am interested in writing in other genres. I am also a director for two companies. I split my time between running my consulting company, writing, and I am halfway through a degree in philosophy at present, having originally qualified with degrees in mechanical engineering and economics. I love to travel and visit exotic places, walk in the mountains, and do cross country running.

Ciprian Rusen I am a 30-year-old from Romania and I consider myself both a geek and a great project manager. So far, I have managed to accomplish most of my dreams. Right now, I am working on becoming a well-rounded author, able to write great books on very diverse subjects. This is my third book and the first which is not about technology. My aim was to summarize what I have learned about achieving dreams in way that's simple, easy to understand and use for as many people as possible. I hope that I have achieved this goal and that you have enjoyed reading this book. If you are interested in learning about other articles and books I have published, don't hesitate to follow me on Twitter at @ciprianrusen or on Google+ at http://gplus.to/ciprianrusen.

Corporate Geek Is a blog where we both write. We started writing together a few years ago. Our articles are mostly about business, project management, how to communicate in the business world and about books we enjoyed reading. If you would like to take a peek, visit: http://corporategeek.info.

ABOUT OUR ILLUSTRATOR

We would like to thank **Laura Dumitru** for the awesome drawings and Illustrations she has created. Her work has helped build even more character and charm into this book. We are proud of the end result and very happy with her contribution.

She would like to say a few words about herself, so that you know more about who she is and how to find her, in case you want to get in touch:

"I've always loved drawing. It is the best way of expressing my ideas and dreams. Drawing has led me to discover and follow a career in visual communication.

I started with a bachelor's degree in graphic design in Bucharest, Romania and a freelance job as a digital illustrator. In 2011 I moved to the Netherlands to follow a Masters in Professional Animation. For 12 months I had the chance to live and reinvent myself both personally and professionally in the very inspiring city of Breda.

As a person who's constantly looking forward to new challenges, I decided to move again. This time to Munich, Germany to do a 6 month internship in interactive design.

I dream of creating graphic novels, animations and other visual works that inspire people and add something new and creative to the world.

If you enjoyed my work throughout this book, don't hesitate to check my online portfolio at http://www.immah.ro. There you will learn more about my work as a digital artist and you can get in touch with me."

ABOUT OUR SPONSOR

Another special thank you goes to **Andrei Chirea**, a young entrepreneur from Bucharest, Romania. He has been a valuable and important influence in making this book. First, he was the one who discovered Laura Dumitru and her awesome work. He proposed that she should become one of our team and he made it happen. Throughout the project he provided guidance from an artistic perspective and valuable input to a few of the chapters we wrote. To top things off, he also covered the costs of the illustrative work and created a few illustrations himself.

We would like to thank him for his personal involvement. His influence has helped us create a book that we believe is both visually pleasing and relevant to our readers.

He would like to share a few words about himself, so that you get to know him better:

"I define myself as both an artist and a programmer. Even though I have a very analytical mind, I consider myself a sensitive person too, open to the needs of those around me. I am passionate about psychology, personal development and NLP (Neuro-linguistic programming). I've done all kinds of activities that have helped me grow and develop as a person, from acting classes to public speaking and NLP courses. This is on top of my daily work as a partner in a company producing casual games since 2007 – Witchhut LLC.

I do my best to help people become happier and I've found this book to be a great tool in doing so. That's why I decided to get involved and help make it happen.

I am also one of the co-founders of The Institute for Happiness, an NGO that aims to measurably raise the level of happiness in Romania. Our goal is to create the necessary awareness to inspire people and help them take full responsibility for their happiness. If you happen to be from Romania, don't hesitate to check us out and join our events."

BECOME A FAN

If you liked this book, go and like it on Facebook and spread the word about it. You can stay up to date with news, events and other interesting updates by following the book's Facebook page. You will also be able to interact with the authors and other people involved in the making of the book.

facebook.com/DreamIt.DoIt.LiveIt

INDEX